GHOST TOWNS

of

IDAHO

THE SEARCH FOR EL DORADO

This is a limited first edition.

Bruce A. Raisch

THE
DONNING COMPANY
PUBLISHERS

GHOST TOWNS

of

IDAHO

THE SEARCH FOR EL DORADO

by Bruce A. Raisch

A Former Red Light District in the
Ghost Town of Silver City

The Donning Company Publishers
184 Business Park Drive, Suite 206
Virginia Beach, VA 23462

Steve Mull, General Manager
Barbara Buchanan, Office Manager
Kathleen Sheridan, Senior Editor
Amanda D. Guilmain, Graphic Designer
Derek Ely, Imaging Artist
Scott Rule, Director of Marketing
Tonya Hannink, Marketing Coordinator
Lori Kennedy, Project Research Coordinator

Steve Mull, Project Director

Library of Congress Cataloging-in-Publication Data

Raisch, Bruce A., 1956–
  Ghost towns of Idaho : the search for El Dorado / by Bruce A. Raisch.
— Limited 1st ed.
      p. cm.
  Includes bibliographical references and index.
  ISBN–13: 978–1–57864–483–4
  1. Ghost towns—Idaho. 2. Idaho—History, Local. 3. Ghost towns—
Idaho—Pictorial works. 4. Idaho—History, Local—Pictorial works. I.
Title.
  F747.R25 2008
  979.6'03—dc22
                                                    2007053020

Printed in the United States of America by Walsworth Publishing Company

DEDICATION

My plan is to dedicate all my western adventures books to a family member who is a U.S. military veteran. As a child, listening to the numerous stories from family members about their various military experiences instilled in me both a sense of duty and a deep interest in history. Many of these relatives were World War II vets, people whom others have called "The Greatest Generation."

It is with great pleasure and honor that I dedicate the third book in this series to one of these men, my uncle, Robert D. Raisch. He is my father's older brother. Uncle Bob enlisted and served with the U.S. Navy during WWII as a radioman. He served on the attack transport USS *Fond du Lac*. Also, during 1949, he was a fire lookout for the U.S. Forest Service in (appropriately) Idaho.

I will always remember him as a kind gentleman.

ACKNOWLEDGMENTS

This book is a reflection and product, not just of thousands of road miles and as many hours of research, but of Idaho and its own people. The beauty of this State, the richness of its history, and the friendliness of its people made this book not only possible but also a lot of fun to research and write.

As always, in a project this size, there are many to thank. I would like to start with the Bureau of Land Management, the National Park Service, the U.S. Forest Service, and the U.S. Postal Service, which were all a pleasure to deal with and very helpful with my research. I lost count of the number of times I called the Elk City Ranger Station. I am grateful for all the help and information provided by Dan Smith. He works out of the Yankee Fork Visitor Center. He has handled a fair number of questions during my visits over the years. He even offered to give me a personal tour of Bayhorse.

I would like to acknowledge and even recommend Salmon River Experience (SRE) for their fine rafting service. Along with the fine professional photography service provided by Salmon River Photos, your adventure on the wonderful, scenic Salmon River (aka "The River of No Return") was an experience of a lifetime.

I would like to thank Karen and Keith Bloodworth. Thanks to Karen for her assistance in photography, and thanks to Keith for just being there and being his fun self. These two often join me for parts of my western adventures. It is Keith with me in the photos of the whitewater rafting trip. We all graduated from the same high school, I was best man at their wedding, and Keith is a fellow military vet. Their great company is always appreciated on my western trips.

A special thanks goes to Charlie Swearingen. While I was in Atlanta, Idaho, he let me interview him for hours on end and was quite informative about old Idaho mining sites and towns. Besides being a true gentleman, Charlie is a "real cowboy" and something of

Pat Cracchiola at the Nez Perce Pass. In the background is Hell's Half Acre Mountain Wilderness Area, a place so rugged that upon seeing it, Lewis and Clark decided to go around it rather than attempt to pass through it.

an artist in his own right. He was but one of many friendly Idaho citizens who freely gave of their time to me. These included small business owners, forest rangers, miners, prospectors, county clerks, residents, and others. Even the names of their towns such as Elk City, Orogrande, and Yellow Pine, tell you much.

The Idaho State Historical Society and the Idaho State Library in Boise were always helpful when asked. The small town museums scattered across the state provided much information. The institutions, no matter what state they are in, are national treasures and should be supported.

I am especially thankful for Steve Mull and Donning Company Publishers believing in my project and me.

Once again, Patricia Cracchiola has assisted and encouraged me in the production of the book. During field research, she has endured much, such as altitude sickness, whistling tornadoes, stampeding wildlife, even my camp cooking. Such dedication does not go unnoticed.

FOREWORD

Because of its great mineral wealth, Idaho is known as the Gem State. With the discovery of this wilderness of mineral wealth came hordes of gold-crazed fortune seekers looking for their El Dorado.

The dictionary states that El Dorado is Spanish for "The Gilded One."

1) A city or country of fabulous riches held by sixteenth-century explorers to exist anywhere from Colorado to South America.

2) A place of fabulous wealth, abundance, or opportunity.

A poet said it better:

EL DORADO

Gaily bedight,
A gallant knight
In sunshine and in shadow,
Had journeyed long,
Singing a song,
In search of El Dorado.

But he grew ol –
This knight so bol –
And o'er his heart a shadow
Fell as he found
No spot of ground
That looked like El Dorado.

And, as his strength
Failed him at length
He met a pilgrim shadow–
"Shadow," said he,
"Where can it be–
This land of El Dorado?"

Many gold prospectors sought their El Dorado in the mountains of Central Idaho.

"Over the Mountains
Of the Moon,
Down the Valley of the Shadow,
Ride, boldly ride,"
The shade replied,
"If you seek for El Dorado!"

Someone who was much better known for another kind of writing wrote the poem. What even fewer are aware of is that he also tried his hand at something else—gold panning. He rushed with many other stampeders in a mad search for gold in French Equatorial Guinea, a place many would end up calling "The Green Hell." Few found gold; even fewer found any fortune. What they did find was jungle, heat, humidity, mosquitoes, dysentery, malaria, typhoid, yellow fever, and death. With these things to recommend it, France would later turn it into a penal colony named Devil's Island.

The name of the gold panner and poet: Edgar Allen Poe.

CONTENTS

This is the road to Idimon. It's also where I stopped for lunch that day.

IDAHO

GHOST TOWNS

his is the third book in a series about ghost town hunting in
the American West. It combines the descriptions and histories
of ghost towns from all over Idaho along with my adventure
and travel stories while visiting these sites. Very often during
a mining boom, a fair number of towns would spring up in a
small area. When the boom went bust, it left a small cluster
of ghost towns. These clusters then divided into their separate
mining districts. This is also how the book is set up.

First, there is a small biography about the district, followed by
the towns in that section. After these clustered towns, there is a

Top: What looks like a road on the map can look like this in person.

Bottom: There are numerous hazards in the backcountry. This full-sized buck fell victim to a cougar.

Months of field research had to be done to gather information and photos for this project. Unless otherwise noted, the ghost towns mentioned in this book were personally visited by me. Often, I would spend the night in the town, or better, its cemetery.

Many towns had more than one name. The names the towns are listed under in this book are what they were best known by. Following the town name is the county in parentheses (i.e., Lemhi). This is accompanied by a biography about the location and sometimes a personal adventure or two.

I have a tendency to visit places with the words "devil" or "hell" in their names, e.g., Devil's Tower or Hell's Half Acre. I am also drawn to places that are said to be an adventure, dangerous, haunted, or hard to get to. I really do enjoy the road less traveled. Then, these adventures, places, and travels are put into my books.

Unless noted otherwise, all photography in this book was done by and copyrighted to me. Wildlife photography used in this book was not taken telescopically; therefore, you can see how close we actually were to each other. Special note: do not approach wildlife; they are "wild" and extremely dangerous. This is but one of a list of things I do that you at home should not try. Another and one of the best safety rules is safety in numbers. Four is considered the minimum number for safety in an outdoor adventure group. I do most of my adventures solo. I do solo mountain climbing, canoeing, spelunking, rock climbing, canyoneering, extreme hiking, and more. I deeply enjoy the wilderness experience in my solitude but also recognize it for the risky behavior it is. My advice is to do what I say and not what I do—go with a group. Take a first aid kit, and let people know where you're going. I do, most of the time.

I do not conform to political correctness. To do so would mean committing historical revisionism. A historian must write what the facts are as he sees them. If he makes any judgments, he must state this is only his judgment. The historian must not cross over to advocacy; to do so means one is no longer a historian but an advocate.

People are a major hazard to ghost towns. This was one of three fire rings with wood from 120-year-old miners' cabins I found at McFadden.

Sometimes I run across a good western legend. If it's germane to the story, I add it to the book but state that it is a legend and not a known fact. As they said in the John Wayne movie, *The Man Who Shot Liberty Valance*: "This is the West. When facts meet the legend, print the legend."

All the books in this series are made in the USA. They are printed in Marceline, Missouri, the hometown of Walt Disney. I've noticed some other books about American ghost towns are printed in Communist China. I'm sure it is cheaper to print them there, but I simply refuse to have my books made by slave labor or to support a totalitarian regime.

If you would like more information about the author, his outdoor adventures, ghost town hunting, or ghost towns of the West, check out the website http://www.theghosttownhunter.com/ or his other two books, *Ghost Towns of Wyoming* and *Ghost Towns and Other Historical Sites of the Black Hills*.

If you have questions or would like to provide any information on additional Idaho ghost town locations, etc., you may email the author about it at bar4916@yahoo.com.

OUTDOOR
IDAHO

I

daho is an outdoor enthusiast's paradise. The beauty of the
state could leave a poet tongue-tied. All one has to do to get a
good view here is to step outside. This is a land of varying and
contrasting landscapes. There are sand dunes to dunebuggy on;
lakes in which to boat, ski, fish, and swim; mountains to climb;
thousands of miles of trails to hike or ride, and so on.

While Idaho is officially known as the Gem State, it is also
unofficially known as the whitewater rafting state. There are
literally thousands of miles of river to float there. I do a river
ride on every trip I take to Idaho. My favorite river in Idaho is
the Salmon River, also known as "The River of No Return." I put
in above Riggins and use SRE (Salmon River Experience) as my
outfitter. They have always shown me a great time. If you decide
to take a raft ride, use a licensed outfitter. There are numerous
rivers and outfitters to choose from in Idaho.

Top: The view from the bow of the raft.

Bottom: In July and August, I camp in mountain passes to take advantage of the cool evenings.

During the summer of 2006, I floated the Salmon River on June 6, which made the date 6/6/06. The spring melt-off was running so high that the river was categorized as Class 5 that day. It was a thrill of a ride.

In 1998, on my first visit to Idaho, I stopped at the Yankee Fork Visitor Center to obtain local information. I had noticed from maps that Idaho was loaded with National Forest land, so I inquired about camping in the area. A very nice lady with a southern accent that surprised me replied, "Oh honey, this is Idaho. You can camp anywhere." As it turns out, she was just about right; you can camp almost anywhere in Idaho. The camping opportunities here are various and numerous. You can do everything from RV-ing to back country primitive camping. One unique and interesting way some people camp in Idaho is by airplane. They land on remote grass airstrips and often set up a tent under the plane's wing. For a real camping adventure in this rugged state, I sometimes rent a mountain from the National Forest Service. Even if not snowed in, the trip to the top can be challenging sometimes. When at the peak, be cautious of lighting strikes. If the clouds allow, you will have a million-dollar view.

In Idaho, it is best if your vehicle is equipped with four-wheel drive. Neither my van nor pickup truck has it, but more than once I wish they did. During my 2006 trip, a rainy spring made mud a frequent problem. My usual strategy when stuck in the mud is to set up camp and wait for the road to dry. Food is never a concern; I carry MREs left over from the first Gulf War in the back of my vehicle. Survival tip: always carry nonperishable food items in your vehicle. Keep safety as a number one priority in your outdoor adventures. Every year, millions visit the North American Rockies, and every year, more than two thousand fail to return.

The big problem—and it was very big in 2007—was fire! More than twenty major forest fires ravaged the state for months that fire season. Damage was extensive. Some of the sites described in this

The view from the mountain I rented near Challis.

book are probably gone. It will take decades for the landscape here to heal. These fires were more than the natural cycle allows. The simple reason is that the forests are too thick. In our urgent push to save the forest, some are hugging it to death. There is a simple solution: thin the forest. When the forest is too thick, the trees become weak and therefore more susceptible to blight, bugs, and droughts. The trees die and become fuel for the next forest fire. Too much fuel means the fire burns too hot and sterilizes the soil beneath. These blazes now have a name: Super Fires. For years, even weeds refused to grow, and rains only produced river-choking mud. This, of course, hurts water quality and kills fish. Add to this the loss of good-paying jobs in the timber industry that have now been exported to Canada and you will see what can come of good intentions. Combine the ingredients of good intentions; the refusal to accept facts you don't like; and abandonment of common sense, and you have the recipe for disaster that became the 2007 western fire season.

A fire-fighting aircraft landing at McCall airport during the severe 2007 forest fire season.

One bright spot in that sad story was watching the men and women of the different Hot Shotz crews from across the nation fight the fires with courage and vigor. They are all volunteers and, in my opinion, very brave. Equally brave are the crews of the fire-fighting aircraft. All that summer, I would see these fine people in the campgrounds, hotels, or restaurants, on the road, or in the air. They were everywhere, and they were needed.

On three different occasions, I volunteered my services to the National Forest Service. I did not expect to actually fight a fire but instead to answer a phone, drive a truck, make lunches, or do other odd jobs, but they weren't prepared to take volunteers.

Another unique Idaho outdoor adventure is a wilderness drive sometimes referred to as "the challenge." It is done on a National Forest road that bisects the largest wilderness area in the lower forty-eight states. North of the road is the Bitterroot Wilderness, and south of the corridor is the Wilderness of No Return, previously known as Hell's Half Acre Mountain Wilderness. On a clear day, you can see Hell's Half Acre Mountain from the Nez Perce Pass. Often, this is where I take friends who have joined one of my western trips because I'd promised to take them to hell.

The combined wilderness area is more than twice the size of the states of Delaware and Rhode Island together. The road used to be part of the Nez Perce Trail and is now called the McGruder Corridor. Its route traverses seven mountain ranges, most of it on gravel or dirt roads. Snow can take until mid-July to melt in the passes. On the one trip I took completely through the corridor, a snow-blocked pass held me up for two days in July. To make matters a little tense, a forest fire had cut the road behind me, and this was the only road.

It is 165 miles between gas stations in Darby, Montana, and Elk City, Idaho, so fill up your gas tank before you head to the corridor. If you take the challenge, go prepared for anything; this is one of the wildest roads in America. The terrain here is so mountainous that when Lewis and Clark saw it from the Nez Perce Pass, they decided to go around it instead of trying to go through it. Do not go solo, as I did; remember, safety in numbers. The National Forest Service puts out a brochure on the McGruder Corridor.

Due to its environment, there are numerous hazards associated with driving in Idaho, and they are not limited to just the back roads. These hazards include ice, deep snow, avalanches, landslides, fallen trees, logging trucks, high winds, wildfires, boulders, or wildlife, like moose on the road. Roads can be closed at any time, and many are closed on a regular basis for the winter season.

Top: During my drive through the McGruder corridor, I frequently had to clear the road of fallen trees, rocks, and even snow.

Bottom: Idaho's back-country roads traverse rugged mountain terrain. The haze in the picture is due to a forest fire in the area.

IDAHO GHOST TOWNS

BOISE BASIN

Golden Age Camp
Idaho City
Pioneerville
Placerville

BUFFALO HUMP MINING DISTRICT

Callender
Concord
Frogtown
Humptown
Orogrande
St. Louis

CENTRAL MOUNTAIN GHOST TOWNS

Big Creek
Czizek
Rocky Bar
Roosevelt
Stibnite
Warren
Yellow Pine

GRAIN SILO GHOST TOWNS

Corral
Drummond
Hill City
Lamont

OWYHEE MOUNTAINS

De Lamar
Dewey
Silver City

OTHER OWYHEE GHOST TOWNS

Fairview
Flint
Ruby City
South Mountain City
Triangle

SALMON AREA GHOST TOWNS

Cobalt
Forney
Gilmore
Hahn
Kingville
Leesburg
May
Merritt
Patterson

Shoup
Yellowjacket

SEVEN DEVILS MOUNTAINS

Cuprum
Decorah
Landore
Placer Basin

SILVER AND LABOR STRIKES

Burke
Delta
Gem
Mace

WHITE KNOB MOUNTAINS

Cliff City
Darlington
Mammoth
White Knob

YANKEE FORK MINING DISTRICT

Bayhorse
Bonanza
Custer
McFadden
Sunbeam
Yankee Fork Dredge

AND ALL THE REST

Atlanta
Banner City
Boulder City (Blaine)
Boulder City (Boundary)
Bridge
Carrietown
Chesterfield
Dixie
Florence
Gnome
Henry
Holbrook
Humphrey
Hunt Station
Idimon
Morrow
Naf
Ovid
Pearl
Sawtooth City
Strevell
Tollgate
Westlake

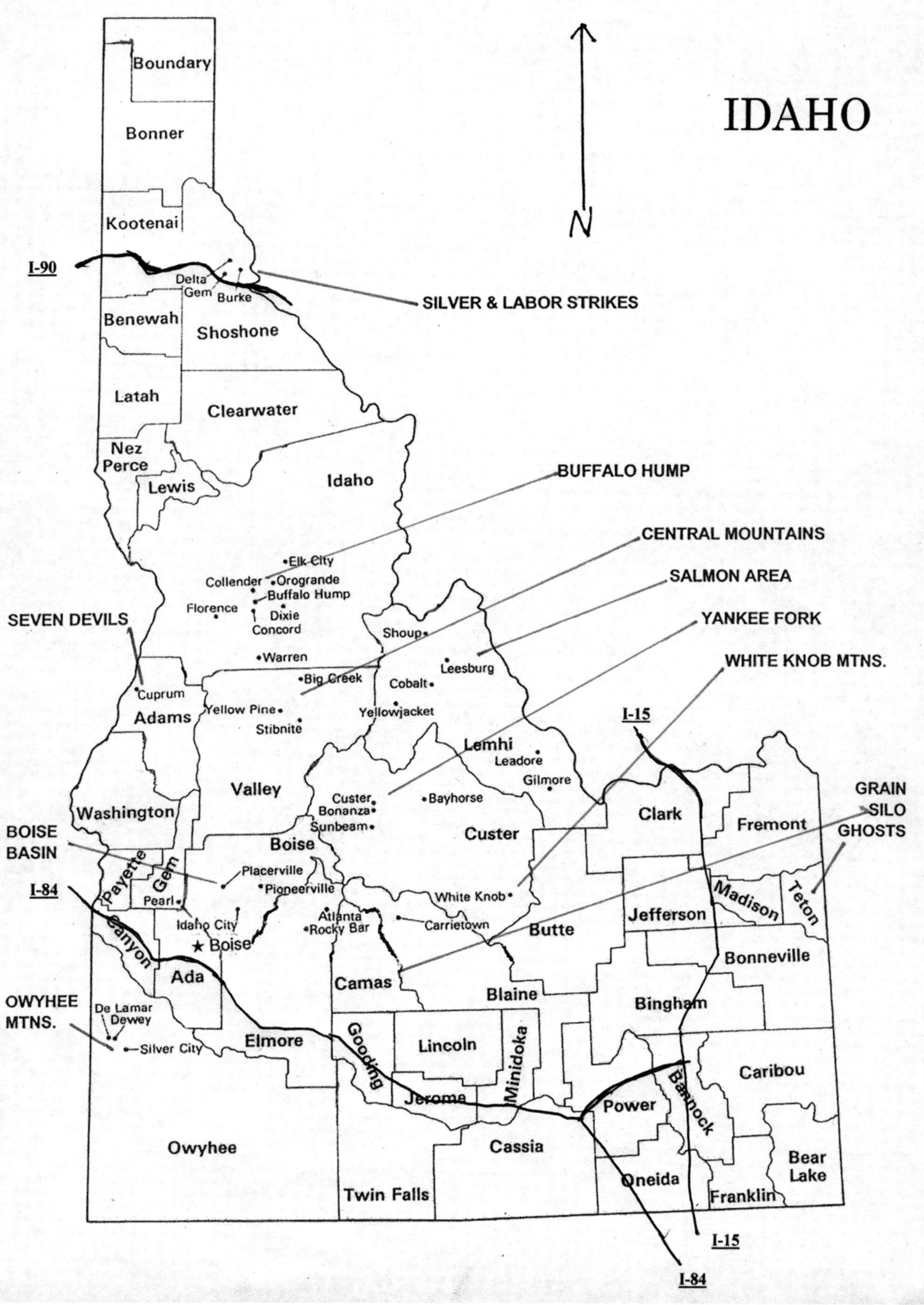

IDAHO
N
Boundary
Bonner
Kootenai
I-90
Benewah
Shoshone
Delta
Gem
Burke
SILVER & LABOR STRIKES
Latah
Clearwater
Nez Perce
Lewis
Idaho
BUFFALO HUMP
Elk City
Collender
Orogrande
Buffalo Hump
Florence
Dixie
Concord
CENTRAL MOUNTAINS
SALMON AREA
Shoup
SEVEN DEVILS
Warren
Big Creek
Leesburg
YANKEE FORK
Cobalt
Cuprum
Yellow Pine
Yellowjacket
WHITE KNOB MTNS.
Adams
Stibnite
Lemhi
I-15
Leadore
Gilmore
Valley
Custer
Bonanza
Bayhorse
Clark
GRAIN
SILO
GHOSTS
Washington
Sunbeam
Custer
Fremont
BOISE BASIN
Boise
Placerville
Pioneerville
White Knob
Jefferson
Madison
Teton
I-84
Payette
Gem
Pearl
Idaho City
Atlanta
Rocky Bar
Carrietown
Butte
Bonneville
Boise
Camas
Blaine
Bingham
Ada
Canyon
OWYHEE MTNS.
De Lamar
Dewey
Silver City
Elmore
Gooding
Lincoln
Minidoka
Caribou
Power
Bannock
Jerome
Cassia
Bear Lake
Owyhee
Twin Falls
Oneida
Franklin
I-15
I-84

Idaho
Ghost Towns

BOISE BASIN

The Boise Basin Gold Rush was the largest and most important one of Idaho and nearly the whole West, for that matter. It began in spring 1862 on a mountain basin above Boise, Idaho, with several placer gold discoveries in Grimes Creek. One major problem, especially for placer mining, was the lack of water. The area is drought-prone and subject to frequent forest fires. The Basin's high altitude meant winters were harsh, and what little water there was would often freeze for the whole season.

From 1862 to 1870, the soil was passionately panned, sluiced, and washed for gold. It was common for miners to pan $100 worth of dust a day; even a flour sack full of local dirt sold for $20.

After 1870, a great deal of the mining here was done hydraulically—that is, they shot giant water cannons at the earth, then sluiced the mud. Some of the old water cannons are on display in Idaho City. This did catastrophic damage to

Numerous abandoned mines dot the basin. They are dangerous; do not enter.

the local environment, the aftereffects of which are still easily seen today. The next modern mining technique, dredging, was equally damaging to the environment. All along the highway leading into Idaho City, both north and south of it, are endless piles of rocks. These are called tailings. A lot of hard-rock mining was also done in the Basin. This kicked into high gear around 1900. Numerous abandoned mine shafts litter the area today. A great deal of gold was taken out of the Basin, and its grand wealth was a positive boon to the rest of the U.S. as a whole.

The Basin is where most of the "firsts" happened, and for a while where most of the people lived in Idaho. For example, this is where Idaho's first newspaper and first race track were. Today, mining still goes on in the area, but logging and tourism are also important industries here now. Most of the land here belongs to the Boise National Forest. Still, there are numerous active mining claims, along with a lot of private property. Please be respectful to all property, public or private.

If you intend to explore the Basin, you should use Idaho City as your jumping-off point. Here, you can easily rally with others, obtain local information and supplies, or just see the town's fine sites.

There were two sites in the Basin that I did not visit—Granite City and Quartzburg. Both locations are either on private property, or access to them is through private property. Since I did not obtain permission to be on these properties, the sites were not visited. Granite City is between Placerville and Quartzburg. It was a small gold mining town on Granite Creek. Remains are said to be one building, one foundation, a sign, and the outline of the old main street. In 1864, the Gold Hill Mine was opened on Gold Hill near Granite Creek. Soon, the town of Quartzburg popped up next to the mine. A twenty-five-stamp mill was installed and was in continuous operation for many years. In 1931, a large forest fire swept the Basin and destroyed almost all of Quartzburg. All that remained was the post office, and, according to some sources, a few houses also survived. The post office was still standing in the late 1970s. There are supposed to be some remains at the site, but I could not confirm this. Evidence of these mining booms litters almost every hill, creek, and gulch in the Basin. If you decide to explore the Basin, you will enjoy discovering old miners' cabins, water flumes, diversion ditches, tailings, and much more with every turn you take. One caution: stay out of the old mines. They are extremely dangerous.

GOLDEN AGE CAMP (Boise)

While not a true ghost town, this old mining camp is one of the precious historic gems of the Boise Basin. This is a fine example of a mining camp, and its current owners are preserving the site. The camp served the Golden Age Mine.

A man named Wells discovered the lode that became the Golden Age mine. Eventually, a Spokane outfit bought up the claim. They spent a great deal of money developing the camp and mining operation.

The camp had two mills, two bunkhouses, a recreation hall, a two-story hotel, an equipment maintenance building, other mine buildings, a dozen homes, sheds, outhouses, and a school named the Diana School. The school taught all the children of the camp and probably the other neighboring camps as well. The teacher was

This was the hotel.

Top: Made with slabs of timber, this miner's cabin predates the camp.

Bottom: Thanks to the owners' preservation efforts, these one hundred-year-old buildings still stand in good condition.

provided with a rent-free cabin. One source claimed there was a post office here, but I have not confirmed that with postal service records. If true, this would classify the site as a town instead of just a mining camp.

At the camp's peak in the early 1900s, seventy-five men were employed here, extracting approximately $3,500 a day in gold. The average pay was $3 a day minus a $1 deduction for room and board if you lived in company housing. Paydays were on Saturday, and there was usually a dance that evening. The dances were held on the second floor of the hotel. On the first floor, there was a company store, dining hall, large kitchen, and a few other rooms.

Over the years, the mining operation had sunk to such a depth that pumps were required to keep it free of water. Even though the gold vein had not pinched out, excessive operating costs caused the mine to close. When operations ceased, the mine rapidly filled with water. Future plans to reopen the mine fell apart when they came up against the cost of pumping out and reshoring the mine.

Although you are in the Boise National Forest, the site itself is on private property. Please respect private property and stay on the road. A caretaker watches the site. On my visit, I was fortunate enough to meet the gentleman. He gave me a tour of the buildings and provided a lot of local information and history.

Most of the camp still stands today. Some of the buildings have been converted to different uses over the years, showing that the camp has been reoccupied at times. The current owners were in the process of cleaning up and repairing many of the buildings. The best is the two-story hotel. Also mixed in with the camp buildings are a few log cabins that predate the Golden Age Mine. These cabins belonged to miners during the Boise Basin boom days.

Even though there is still small-scale mining in the area, the combination of high development costs and environmental concerns have prevented the reopening of the Golden Age Mine. The camp is about a mile east of Grimes Pass. Caution: the road at the north end of this pass has a steep gradient.

The second time I drove down the pass, I surprised a fox in the road. He ran off the road on the downhill side, and it was so steep, the sure-footed fox ended up cartwheeling down the mountain. The fox survived the fall; I encountered it in the road a second time near the bottom of Grimes Pass.

IDAHO CITY (Boise)

This is not a ghost town; instead, it is a western tourist town, and one that is well worth the visit. Founded in 1862, it was first called Bannock City; later, the name was changed to Idaho City. There are numerous old wood and brick buildings remaining from the boom period. The boom years were 1865–88. After that, the town faded but never died. From the late 1880s to the early 1940s, hydraulic mining was done here. Water cannons called "Water Giants" were used to wash away the earth. The resulting mud was then sluiced for gold dust. It produced millions in gold but devastated the land. You can still see the effects for miles along Highway 21. More history on Water Giants and many other things can be found in Idaho City. The place is much like an outdoor museum with restaurants and gift shops.

Downtown Idaho City.

A handful of buildings are claimed to be haunted by pioneer spirits; my favorite is the Idaho Hotel. There is a beautiful and historic western cemetery in town. This graveyard was first plotted in 1863 and is also alleged to be haunted.

Some of the other historic sites in town are the Masonic Temple, Miners Exchange (one of the oldest buildings in the state), Idaho World Building (home of Idaho's oldest newspapers), Idaho City Park (displays a jail, log cabin, and old mining equipment), St. Joseph's Catholic Church (built in 1867), and the list goes on. My favorite place to visit in town is Diamond Lil's, a restaurant and saloon. It used to be a general store in the boom days. The place is almost a

museum in its own right, and this creates a wonderful atmosphere. The food and service have always been very good on my visits, and the owners are always willing to chat and provide local information with a smile. Idaho City is an easy drive north of Boise and is shown on the state highway map. Caution: Highway 21 is narrow and winding.

PIONEERVILLE (Boise)

The first town of any consequence to spring up in the rich Boise Basin had an interesting birth. In fall 1862, a band of prospectors led by J. Marion Moore found placer gold on upper Grimes Creek. On October 7, the merry little band set up camp and christened it Pioneer City. The panners were so excited about their finds that they lost track of the seasons, their supply levels, and the local Indians. The Indians, on the other hand, knew that fall was approaching, had stored food for the winter, and were watching the miners. Right from the very start, hostile Indians were a major problem for this gold camp.

When the miners finally realized that they didn't have enough supplies, both winter and the hostile Indians were tightening their grip on the camp. The men decided upon a plan that wouldn't force

Left: Main Street Pioneerville.
Above: In the trees just beyond the town are miles of dredge tailings.

them to give up their gold strike: they formed two groups. The first group gathered the pack animals and headed to Lewiston for supplies and to post their claims. The other group stayed behind and built a small stockade. The miners called it Fort Haynes. Then they sat tight inside the stockade until the supply train returned six weeks later. Upon the first group's return, everyone staked out claims on the creek. When others followed after the supply train, they found all the good ground staked out and already claimed. They complained that Moore's group had hogged all the good land. Because of this, the place would become known as Fort Hogem. Soon, this was shortened to Hogem. Many gold panners reacted to the so-called land-hogging by moving downstream on Grimes Creek and starting the town of Centerville. Soon, it too, became a boomtown. Later, the name was officially changed from Pioneer City to Pioneerville. The entire Basin began to fill with businessmen and miners, whether they went to Centerville, Pioneer City, or someplace else.

The whole Basin boomed, and Pioneerville boomed with the area. It had the Basin's first post office, which was established in 1864. The population, depending on the source you quote, peaked between 2,000 and 2,743. When the placers started to thin out, so did the population. Soon, miners drifted to richer diggings in the

Top: The collapsed remains in front of the house was a two-seat outhouse. The house had electrical power, probably from the hydroelectric plant there.

Bottom: Remains like this foundation cover a large area around Pioneerville.

Basin. Dredging operations started a second boom here. Grimes Dam and a power plant were built on the South Fork of the Payette River to provide electricity for the dredges and the mining towns. Today a handful of people still live in the town. Dredge tailings are everywhere. The National Forest road to here from Centerville is the old stagecoach route. One dredge remained here until the 1970s.

PLACERVILLE (Boise)

Started in 1862 as a placer gold mine camp, Placerville is appropriately named. Fed by gold dust and not hemmed in by mountain walls, the place mushroomed in size. By fall 1863, there were more than one hundred buildings and 3,254 people. The business here included at least five blacksmiths, five meat markets, seven restaurants, thirteen saloons, and three hotels, plus numerous boardinghouses and stores.

Dry summers caused water shortages not only for gold panning but also even for drinking. Within two years, a series of diversion canals were dug and solved the problem. Panning continued through 1870, after which it was mostly replaced by hard-rock mining operations. A major forest fire leveled most of Placerville in 1899.

Starting around 1910, dredging operations created another small boom. This was followed by yet one more small boom during the high gold prices of the 1930s. In 1942, the U.S. government required the closing of all nonessential mining. This was the final nail in the coffin of gold mining for the area.

Top: A barn or livery stable.

Middle: A lot of Placerville looks like this.

Bottom: The town square with the famous Magnolia Saloon.

The Emmanuel Episcopal Church still holds services. It is one of many well-preserved historical buildings in Placerville.

This town has a small year-round population of fourteen. Services available here are a small general store with gas pumps and a pay phone. Common elsewhere, but unique in the pioneer West, it has a town square instead of the usual main street. In the center is a grass courtyard with a flagpole proudly flying the American flag. The buildings surrounding the square vary greatly in construction, including stone, log, whip-sawed lumber, and modern. False fronts are common. There are a few original "boom" buildings here. Many have been converted to summer cottages, and two are now museums. One original structure is now used as the City Hall. The Magnolia, one of the town's original saloons, still stands today as a museum. There is also the old mercantile building and the large Masonic hall to view. There are a fair number of homes or cabins here. Some are vacant, others seasonal, even fewer full-time residences. Although most buildings postdate the 1899 fire, they are still, for the most part, rather old.

My visit here was before the tourist season started, so everything was closed. On the road there, you see numerous other old buildings and dredge tailings. Just outside of town on a hill to the southeast are the Placerville cemetery and reservoir.

The cemetery is worth the side trip. It contains much information on its numerous and sometimes unique headstones. It is well maintained and still used. It is a place where you can easily forget time because time has forgotten it. The reservoir is directly below the graveyard and is still in use after one hundred years. It is used to provide water pressure for the town's hydrants. The system was built in response to the 1899 fire.

Placerville is north of Boise, northwest of Idaho City, and marked on the state highway map. It is on an all-weather gravel road, and road signs mark the way there. These facts do not guarantee that you won't get stuck or lost. The area can be buried in snow during the winter, and the road has numerous intersections, many of which are not marked. If you do visit, you will find the place both historically interesting and just plain beautiful.

The cemetery at Placerville is historic and well maintained.

BUFFALO HUMP MINING DISTRICT

This was the last major pioneer gold rush in the lower forty-eight states. It is strange that so little has been written about it. The district gets its name from Buffalo Hump Mountain, which to some resembles the back of a buffalo.

Gold was first discovered here in summer 1862, but a severe blizzard on the Fourth of July drove all the prospectors out of these mountains. The discovery seems to have been forgotten, as prospectors did not return until 1898. On August 8 of that summer, two prospectors, Charles H. Robbins and Kenneth B. Young, accidentally discovered gold while deer hunting. Their discovery set off one of the last great gold stampedes. At first, the new mining district was called the Robbins, then the Concord District, but most miners called it the Buffalo Hump from the start. The miners also had problems from the start: this is some of the most rugged and remote terrain in America.

There were no roads or trails to the Hump. Two pack trails were blazed up to the mountain, one from Orogrande and the other from Grangeville. In 1900, a rough wagon road, in some places hewn by hand from the rock, was completed from Orogrande. In 1903, a telephone line followed the same route. This development was too little and too late. The rush was over by 1904. Other problems hampering development on the plateau were too few carpenters and sawmills. After a few years of the rush, deforestation was added to the list of problems.

At first, like many rushes, there was great hope here. People thought the Buffalo Hump was a mountain of gold, a true El Dorado. At the height of the rush, there were seven thousand people in about eight square miles. At eight thousand feet, winters on the plateau were long and hard, with snow sometimes staying on the ground year-round. Food could not be grown here; it had to be brought in. One simple way to move a lot of food to the plateau was cattle drives.

The road to the left goes to Badger, the road to the right the Buffalo Hump. Both were closed due to forest fires.

Over steep mountain ranges, five thousand head of cattle were driven over some of the most difficult, rugged, yet scenic land the West has to offer. The stories and scenes of this rush beg of an old-time John Wayne western. It seems that nobody in Hollywood wants to make money anymore; otherwise, they would have produced a movie about this place.

The boomers here were doomed to failure. There was plenty of gold, but the ore was low grade and not free-milling. Development was both difficult and expensive, and the reasons were simple: it was hard to get the ore out of the ground, hard to get the gold out of the ore, and almost impossible to get anything in or out of the region at a profit. Transportation was the Achilles heel of the Buffalo Hump rush.

An interesting character and the prime promoter of this boom was Charles Sweeney. He was and is a controversial figure. I found more written about him than I did about the Buffalo Hump and its gold rush. Mr. Sweeney, a second-generation Irish immigrant, was a self-made business entrepreneur. He had come west to seek his fortune after the Civil War and was successful. He jumped headlong into the mining industry, doing prospecting, promoting, speculating, and, some say, manipulating. He invested a lot of money into the Buffalo Hump region and got others to invest even more. Callendar was his company town. He had the road built to the plateau. He consolidated a majority of the holdings on the Hump and issued stock certificates. Then in 1903, just before the boom went bust, he sold all his holdings there.

The boom continued through 1904, then dropped off dramatically. Mining continued here on a small scale through at least 1914. The 1930s brought another spat of activity that lasted into summer 1942. Scattered remains spanning fifty years were spread over the whole plateau. Mixed with this was newer vacation-home construction. Real estate ads in Grangeville showed that homes on the Buffalo Hump are expensive.

The last eight miles of road to the Hump are a nightmare and frequently damage ATVs. During summer 2007, a blaze named the "Concord Fire" burned for months on the plateau; what now remains, I could not say. Fire also hit the plateau previously during 2003. Special note: mosquitoes can be bad here in the summer.

Even though the Buffalo Hump is totally surrounded by wilderness, much of the land on the plateau is private property; please be respectful.

CALLENDER (Idaho)

This was one of the principal boomtowns of the rush. It started as a collection of tents called "Hill's Camp." Mr. Hill was the superintendent of a number of mines there. In April 1899, a building boom started, and the camp's name was changed. Callender was named after Thomas O. Callender of New York, one of Charles Sweeney's brokers. He had accompanied Mr. Sweeney previously to see the mines in the area. The town was the principal center for the Crackerjack, North Star, Vesuvius, and Wiseboy mines and three stamp mills. It became the headquarters for Mr. Sweeney's mining operations at the Buffalo Hump. As such, there was a large company store, hospital, assay office, and several large warehouses in a row. By 1900, the town had a post office and bank. The bank handled the payroll for a number of the mines here, including the Big Buffalo and Kerrimack. Reportedly, these two mines had a combined payroll of more than five hundred men at their peak. Photos of the period show a number of well constructed two- and three-story frame buildings.

Starting in January 1900, ore from the Vesuvius ran over a twenty-two-hundred-foot tramway to its own mill. The Crackerjack ran a ten-stamp mill. They tried to use waterpower, but the harsh winters froze over the streams, thus cutting off the power. There was another ten-stamp mill named the Callender Mill. The Wiseboy Mine owned and operated a sawmill here. It was a good business; demand for lumber was high during the boom.

A fire in August 1903 destroyed a large section of the town, and it was saved only with the liberal and aggressive use of dynamite. The post office and the town were in continuous use until at least 1914.

The town's location in Callender Canyon allowed for the use of mountain streams to provide power for its mills. It also made the place vulnerable to avalanches. A rough wagon road was built from Orogrande in 1900. In places, the road had to be hewn by hand from the rock. It is the same route used today as a National Forest road to the Buffalo Hump, #233. It is an extremely rough road, more like a jeep trail. In 1903, a telephone line reached here from Orogrande.

In my research, I found four different spellings for this town—either one or two "l"s, combined with an "a" or an "o." I believe "Callender" is the correct spelling.

After the Concord fire, this sign outside old Orogrande is all that might remain now of the ghost towns on the Buffalo Hump.

CONCORD (Idaho)
ALTITUDE 8,050 FEET

This was the southernmost of a string of five boomtowns built during the initial development of the Buffalo Hump Mining District. It is located on the Buffalo Hump mountain plateau, about two miles south of the peak. The site has been used off and on for more than a century.

An ore vein and a mine exploiting it were named Concord. The town got its name from the mine. John Leffler founded both the mine and the town in 1898. It was also the base camp for the much larger Jumbo Mine to the south. At first, Concord was probably no more than a collection of tents. Construction would boom by spring 1899. By 1900, the town had a post office. Other buildings here consisted of an assay office, butcher shop, several houses, mine buildings, and a large hotel with a bar. A visitor in 1939 found these buildings still standing and occupied by seasonal miners who were working the Concord Mine.

In the early 1930s, a small airstrip was constructed next to the town to help with the transportation of supplies for the mining community. This airfield rests at an altitude of eighty-one hundred feet. The first pilots to use the airstrip had to be very brave or very crazy. Flying a biplane in the mountains, then trying to land it on the side of a mountain with little or no landing or navigational aids has to be the definition for one of the two words.

Besides the Concord, the town also served the Ajax and Atlas mines. A small graveyard, the only one that appears on the National Forest map of the area, is just west of town.

Census and postal records show only small populations here (ten in 1900). Most miners stayed in tents, and then only seasonally. The area is full of alpine marshes, ensuring a plentiful supply of mosquitoes in the summer. A forest fire in 2003 and another fire in 2007 called the "Concord Fire" caused some damage. Although

surrounded by a designated National Wilderness, the site is on
private property.

FROGTOWN (Idaho)

Located one mile below the peak of Buffalo Hump on its east side are
the bare remains of a small gold mining town. The first settlement
here was a mining camp that appeared in 1861 during the initial gold
rush. A severe summer snowstorm drove everybody out during July
1862. It popped up again in spring 1899. At first, it was just called
Buffalo, after the mountain peak that dominates the area. Later, its
name was changed to Frogtown (date unknown). Frogtown got its
name from croaking frogs in an alpine swamp next to the town. This
bog and a creek running through it may have been the main water
source of the town. This was a true boomtown of log structures and
tents. All but one source referred to this place by the second name. At
one time, the town had a restaurant, two saloons, a general store, and
a bakery. More than one source has referred to Frogtown as the adult
entertainment center for the miners of Humptown.

Mountain climbers reported remains still visible at this location in
2003. They claim on their website that the town had brothels in its
boom period. Frogtown died with the end of the 1898–1903 rush.

This town would have principally served both the Atlas Mine and
Mill. Also surrounding the town were the Lucky Lode, Big Buffalo,
Vesuvius, and the Lare Mines. Frogtown was situated on a western-
facing slope of the plateau about midway between Humptown and
Concord. This ghost town is the only one on the plateau entirely on
National Forest land.

HUMPTOWN (Idaho)
ALTITUDE 7,850 FEET

Started as a tent camp in August 1898 next to the Big Buffalo Mine,
this was a boomtown by early 1899. It was still mostly tents at that
time.

Frogtown and Concord competed with Humptown for attention from miners of the Big Buffalo and boomers.

Humptown had a couple of advantages over the other two towns. It was closer to the mine, and it lay on the spot where the supply trail from Grangerville emptied onto the mountain plateau. Later, this trail became one of two rough wagon roads built into the Hump. To serve the miners, at one time the town had at least five saloons, one dance hall, two hotels, and a livery stable with a barn. During 1913 or slightly before, most of the original town burned down due to a forest fire.

The Big Buffalo Mine had a ten-stamp rock-crushing mill. The mine shut down on March 19, 1903. Since then, it has operated off and on, and then only on a limited basis.

A photo from 1902 shows Humptown to be a community of frame or log buildings and tents. The buildings, some two or three stories, were not as well constructed or finished as those of the company town of Callender.

(OLD) OROGRANDE (Idaho)
ALTITUDE 2,520 FEET

Orogrande was founded in the 1860s as a placer mining camp, and its name appropriately means "great gold" in Spanish. By 1870, the population had ballooned to more than fifteen hundred whites and several Chinese. The town had seven stores, seven saloons, three boardinghouses, two express offices, and more than one hundred other buildings. Lack of sawmills in the area led to high lumber prices. Construction was rough at best in this town.

The placer fields started to play out during 1871. By spring 1872, the population was two hundred, and half of these were Chinese. That winter turned extra rough, and almost all the white miners left. This left about one hundred Chinese miners at the site, reworking old claims. During winter 1879, Indians attacked the Chinese, and most of the town was burned. An unknown number of Chinese were

Top: The Colgrove Hotel.
Bottom: The livery stable.

killed, but two survived by hiding in a cellar. The town would come back, although it would never regain its size of 1870.

Of course, the place was never called "old" while it was occupied. New Orogrande is about a mile northeast of the old site. Both are marked on the National Forest service map of the area. Orogrande is in an isolated location even by Idaho standards, and it served two even more isolated mining communities. Placer gold had been panned around the area since 1861. The discovery of quartz ore in the area gave the community of Orogrande a rebirth. When a gold rush in 1898 to nearby Buffalo Hump started, the town grew as a supply and transportation center. It was already a freight and stage station for the Badger Mine and Mill to the south. In 1899, Mr. Colgrove built a hotel, post office, and store to serve the new rush. The hotel was named after him, and all three businesses were running by August.

Around 1900, major quartz mining added to the local economy. The two principal mines were the Orogrande and the Penman/Homestake. The Orogrande was composed of a large glory hole and a few short tunnels. In 1902, a twenty-stamp mill next to the mine—and a few years later, a cyanide treatment plant—was added. The Homestake Mine was five miles northeast of Orogrande near the crest of a high mountain divide. It had a mining camp attached to it.

Orogrande itself lay astride a wagon road. The two mining districts were above the town in the mountains and about a dozen miles away. Over time, two rough wagon roads to the mines were built by hand into the mountains, thus turning Orogrande into a minor road junction. Soon, the town became a trade and service center for those mining districts. The boom on the Buffalo Hump plateau lasted until 1904. After that, mining there continued on a small scale until 1914 and the beginning of WWI. By then, the town had shrunk to ninety-seven people and the school to sixteen students. A small amount of mining returned to the area after the war.

Top: The electrical hookup shows this cabin has been reoccupied in more modern times.

Bottom: This lodge in new Orogrande appeared closed and may have once been a church.

The town of Orogrande muddled through until the next mining resurgence hit the area during the Depression. The 1930s saw the birth of other industries for the area. People started to use the place to camp, fish, and hunt. Also, the Mt. Vernon dredge operated nearby on the Crooked River until 1941.

Orogrande is marked on the state highway map. It is located southwest of Elk City on the Crooked River Road. This is a good all-weather gravel road. What's left of Old Orogrande is the Colgrove Hotel, the livery barn, four cabins, a shed, an outhouse, one converted seasonal cabin, a National Forest historical marker, and numerous collapsed structures. There are several good National Forest campgrounds in the area, plus a couple million acres of National Forest to do primitive camping in. There is a dirt airstrip north of town that was built in the 1930s and is still used today.

Just outside of town, the road splits. The branch to the right climbs and dead-ends on the Buffalo Hump Mountain plateau. The road to the left also climbs a mountain on its way to the old mining camp of Badger.

This is the Orogrande Airstrip, still in use.

ST. LOUIS (Idaho)
ALTITUDE 8,000 FEET

St. Louis was a name given to a particular ore vein: a mine, a prospect pit, and a mill. One book states that it was operating in 1940, so it would not have been part of the boom period. It would have had an adjacent camp by the same name such as Jumbo did, or maybe even a real town. Its location shows on both the National Forest and U.S. Geographical Survey area maps. These maps show a number of buildings, mines, and ore pits with the name "St. Louis" ambiguously in the center of them. The site is situated about halfway between Concord and Jumbo Camp. The area is split evenly between private and National Forest land. The Concord airstrip is nearby and could have been utilized by this site.

According to the *Lewiston Tribune*, supplies were parachuted to miners here during May 1942. The winter had been severe, and the miners were running out of food and were still snowed in.

Not long after that, all mining here ceased for the duration of WWII. It had been declared by the U.S. government to be nonessential to the war effort. Major development never resumed. The environment is a mixture of forest, alpine lakes, and bogs.

In Idaho, small aircraft and back-country airstrips are often used for camping, fishing, hunting, and whitewater trips.

CENTRAL MOUNTAIN TOWN SITES

With a bad case of "you can't get there from here," this area is exactly what it says it is: mountainous and in the dead center of the state. There are more than a half dozen ghost towns in this part of the state.

These towns have a number of things in common. They were all mining towns. Each one has seen much busier days. All are remote, even by Idaho standards, with a tendency to be closed off by snow for the entire winter. This was the case even at the towns' "peaks." One more thing: all were threatened by large forest fires in summer 2007.

BIG CREEK (Valley)

A prospecting party led by James Reardon and L. M. Johnson discovered gold at Big Creek in June 1884. They organized the Alton Mining District on June 15, 1885, and in a matter of weeks, 150 prospectors had shown up to pan gold. Both placer and tunnel mining began immediately but on a limited basis.

Old photos show a wagon and stagecoach station here in 1900. The small sister community of Logan City was started in summer 1904. It was near Logan Creek, from which it got its name. There were a saloon, store, butcher shop, and house. A four-stamp mill arrived in 1906. Later, the town acquired a post office under the name Edwardsburg. The new name came via W. A. Edwards, owner of much of the town, land, and mines in the area. The mill produced until at least 1911. This was Big Creek's only competition. Edwardsburg's location is marked on the National Forest map of the area.

Today, Big Creek has a very small year-round population. There is an airstrip, the Big Creek store, the Big Creek Ranger Station, and a number of seasonal cabins. Big Creek is shown on most Idaho road maps.

CZIZEK (Idaho)

Deep in the remote Marshall Lake Wilderness Area is the gold-mining ghost of Czizek. Mining in the Marshall Lake area goes back to at least 1902. The largest mine in the area was the Golden Anchor; later, the small town of Czizek would evolve around this mine. A website states a deposit was discovered here around 1902 by John Fox and Phoenix Briggs, while a book gives 1915 as the year and furnishes no names for its discovery. The whole place is dotted with numerous abandoned mines that still show on maps today. In the same valley with the Golden Anchor mine was the Sherman Howek, the Kinerly, which is situated next to a small yet beautiful mountain lake, and four other major mines. Almost two dozen more mines are nearby in the mountains surrounding this central hub.

The Golden Anchor had a schoolhouse and store and served as the local headquarters. The mine was later owned and operated by Leif Holte and Jay Cziezek. Mr. Cziezek had previously been a mine inspector for the state of Idaho. The mine was closed for an extended time. The United Verde Extension Mining Company of Jerome, Arizona, invested a large amount of money in the mine during the 1930s, and it was reopened in 1940.

A post office was opened here on September 27, 1940, under the name of Czizek, thus becoming the only town in the mining district. It was to be a short-lived honor. When WWII began to impact America, numerous mines in the country and especially in the Marshall Lake area that weren't essential to the war effort were forced to close. The post office closed on May 3, 1942, and most miners had left the area by that fall. Since then, the area has reverted to wilderness. The remains of a power plant are on nearby White Creek.

Roads in the area, when they even exist, are rough and steep. Snow is frequent, heavy, and slow to melt. A four-wheel drive vehicle and the ability to read topographical maps are needed to reach this site. Remains at Czizek are the mine, mill, and a number of shacks.

Due to the steepness of the area, many buildings here were built on stilts. When the legs gave out of these structures, they fell to the ground with a shattering effect. It is hard to tell what was what. The location of the Golden Anchor Mine is shown on the Nez Perce National Forest map. If you go, do so for the spectacular scenery and the adventure. The whole area was threatened by wildfire during 2007.

ROCKY BAR (Elmore)

This town was established during December 1863 by H. T. P. Comstock as part of Idaho's initial gold rush. There were numerous large mines nearby on Bear Creek, leading to rapid growth for Rocky Bar. In less than a year, the town grew to twenty-five hundred. When Alturas County was created during 1864, Rocky Bar was made the county seat and kept that honor until 1881.

Rocky Bar is one of a handful of ghost towns for sale in Idaho.

Top: The barrel implores motorists to drive slowly.

Bottom: Finding safes in ghost towns is common. Finding one with its door still on is unheard of.

At first, quartz milling was done with the use of arrastras, and by 1864, there were fifty-three of them serving the diggings in the area. When a road was built into the town, freight wagons hauled in several stamp mills. The largest of these was the fifty-stamp mill at the Elmore Mine. With the introduction of these mills, production of ore grew by leaps and bounds.

Chinese miners moved in between 1870 and 1880. A large Chinatown was built along the banks of Steel Creek. A newspaper, the *Elmore Bulletin*, was published here from June 1, 1889, to June 4, 1892. On September 1, 1892, most of Rocky Bar, including Chinatown and the county courthouse, burned down in a savage fire. The residents rebuilt most of the town, and mining continued. Dredge mining was done in the area during the 1920s.

One pioneer-day story attached to Rocky Bar is the tale of Peg Leg Annie. Annie was a madam who ran at least two houses. One day in May 1898, she decided to walk one of her girls from Atlanta to Rocky Bar. It is a long walk, and there was already snow on the ground. Night found them in a mountain pass near Atlanta Summit with a blizzard pounding down on them. They became trapped in the snow and hugged each other as their only protection from the storm. The blizzard raged for two days. When the women failed to show up after three days, a search party was organized at Rocky Bar. The search party found Annie crawling and mumbling incoherently. The girl, Dutch Em, was found frozen to death. Annie survived, but her legs had to be amputated, earning her the nickname "Peg Leg." Peg Leg Annie became a popular local figure who was known for her works of charity as well as for her services as a madam.

In the mid-1970s, there were still a few residents here, along with one bar and grill. It occupied a one hundred-year-old structure that was once the schoolhouse. On my first visit in 2005, the town was vacant and for sale. I spent the night there. While investigating the site, I had a startling encounter there. I was just sticking my head into the doorway of the old hotel when a loud stomping noise

The first step out the second-story door had to be eye-opening.

became audible. My eyes had not become accustomed to the dark room; still, instinct took over. I backed away and to the side of the doorway. At that moment, a large mule deer came bolting out. Large is pretty much the only size they come in. It brushed against me, knocking me down in the process. During 2007, I saw a real estate ad still listing the town for sale. The asking price was $250,000 and included mineral rights.

Remains here are a little more than a half dozen buildings. These include a small two-story hotel and a cabin rumored to have belonged to "Peg Leg Annie." There are foundations, debris, outhouses, and at least one safe without its door. Construction here showed these buildings had been reoccupied several times. Many of these town's buildings have been removed to Atlanta.

On my visit, I was greeted by a streaming cloud of monarch butterflies. They were passing through the area while on a migration. The sight was both beautiful and bizarre.

ROOSEVELT (Valley)

This town was born during January 1902 and named for the very popular president of the time, Teddy Roosevelt. It was a true boomtown. The Idaho Land and Loan Company of Boise laid out and promoted the town site. It was strung out along Monumental Creek, and lots sold for $100 up. The fact that the place was buried in winter snow and that the miners already there were in danger of starving in their tents did not hinder the promoters from running newspaper ads in Boise singing the town's praises. It was part of the Thunder Mountain gold rush. This, with the Buffalo Hump, was the last major frontier gold rush in Idaho or even the lower forty-eight states, for that matter. The Thunder Mountain Rush was the smaller and even more remote of the two. It produced only two town sites of any longevity; Roosevelt was one of them. The rush got its name from the mountain on which the gold was discovered. The mountain got its name from the echo effect that occurred when lighting struck the higher peaks nearby.

Eventually, its location next to Thunder Mountain and its being the most heavily traveled trail to the mines led to the town's temporary success. In July 1902, the town acquired a post office. Roosevelt soon became the central hub of this short-lived gold rush. In 1904, a wagon road and a telephone line were completed to Roosevelt. The road allowed for some heavy mining equipment to be brought in to the mines of Thunder Mountain. These improvements gave a huge boost to the local economy. The prosperity lasted only a couple more years. Except for a few high-grade pockets, the ore here turned out to be of low grade and expensive to extract. After 1907, most mines and mills in the area closed. Mining continued in the area on a small scale until the late 1920s, but did so without the town of Roosevelt. The town was completely destroyed by a natural disaster.

On May 30, a huge mudslide started in a draw south of the Dewey Mine. It only flowed at the pace of a man, but the huge mass flowed for thirty-six hours and swept everything before its path. It flowed into Mule Creek until it met Monumental Creek and deposited its mass against a mountainside. This formed a natural dam and backed up Monumental Creek into a lake that would later become known as Roosevelt Lake. The lake grew slowly in size until it swallowed up the whole town. There were only about twenty or thirty people left in the town at the time, and they all hurried to remove what they could to higher ground before the lake swallowed it. They worked frantically but were not able to save everything, and for years afterward, supply-strapped miners would try to retrieve items from the site.

What little remains of Roosevelt is under the lake. For decades, logs from the old cabins occasionally would float to the lake surface. When the lake is low and clear, outlines of some structures can be seen. Divers have been known to explore the site, but this has its hazards. The lake is extremely cold and its bottom deep in silt. Diving near the bottom easily clouds the water and cuts visibility to near zero.

This was probably the most isolated and remote ghost town location I visited. If you visit the site, go with a full gas tank and a pickup or SUV. The roads after Yellow Pine should be taken only in dry weather. The roads get even rougher and steeper after Stibnite. When you reach the Thunder Mountain, you will find the scenery as spectacular as it is rugged. There were numerous mining ruins on the mountain until the late 1970s. A number of tramways and mills were still standing. Since then, time and the 2007 forest fire season have taken a very heavy toll.

STIBNITE (Valley)

During the rush to Thunder Mountain, gold was discovered on the upper portion of the South Fork of the Salmon. As usual with Central Idaho, this discovery was in a remote area with very difficult terrain for settlement or transportation. Because of these difficulties, the area was slow to develop. Records show gold and antimony claims weren't posted until 1914. Because of wartime shortages, there was a short mining boom for mercury here in 1918. Full-scale mining development began in 1927 after F. W. Bradley bought the mines. Major production of antimony and gold began in 1932. Important tungsten deposits were put into production during 1944.

Mining company buildings on the edge of the glory hole mine.

A raging flood has flattened most of this mining camp.

By the end of the war, Stibnite was the largest domestic producer of tungsten at that time. It accounted for 80 percent of domestic tungsten production. It was so important to the war effort that the mine was subsidized by the federal government, and mining there counted as military service.

At first, most mining here was done by tunneling. Later, during WWII, a rather large glory hole was dug. It is still there, to be seen today. The mines closed in 1952 after the federal government stopped stockpiling domestic tungsten.

Stibnite had been a company town complete with company housing and company stores; it even had a hospital. The population numbered several thousand. When the mine closed, the town mostly closed. Most of the houses were trucked out over the hazardous mountain road on large flatbed trailers to Yellow Pine or McCall. Most have been sold, but some may still be purchased at Yellowpine. They are neat and tidy but small—typical company housing. Photo records show the town had a large three-story frame recreation hall. It had a café, pool table, and nightclub. It was once the social center of town. Now almost everything is gone. Heavy metals from mine

Top: Partial remains of a few structures still stand.
Bottom: This building appeared to once have contained a boiler.

tailings caused this place to be declared an EPA "superfund" cleanup site. Most of the town site was leveled and covered with a four-story-high hill of dirt and rock. I spotted one early-period log cabin in the woods, and the airfield with a tattered windsock is all that remains of the actual town. I even used the old airstrip as my campsite for the evening. Below the town site, there is much left of the mining operation. The huge mill was mostly dismantled, but the shell of the building remains. The mountain valley narrows considerably here, and many flattened buildings show signs of being knocked down by a raging flood. These are the remains of the Yellow Pine Mine, the mill site, and two mining camps or centers named Midnight and Monday Camp. This information comes from a National Forest service map of the "Wilderness of No Return."

When precious-metal prices increased in the 1970s, Canadian Superior installed a pilot plant to test the ore here during 1978. By 1980, the company had invested $10 million in developing a major new operation. Nothing much came of it. Stibnite still shows on numerous maps, even though it really isn't there anymore. The road to the site should be attempted only during dry weather.

WARREN (Shoshone)
ALTITUDE 5,888 FEET

Although there is a small year-round population here (nine to sixteen), Warren is still considered a ghost town, and a great one at that. The place is a virtual open-air museum with its own posted walking tour.

History starts here in summer 1862, when a party of three miners from Florence, including one James Warren, discovered placer gold in Slaughter Creek. A crudely constructed log building was erected at the mouth of the creek to store the group's pack train of goods. Around this site quickly sprang up the camp of Richmond. These humble beginnings earn the title of the fifth-oldest mining community in the state of Idaho. The name Richmond came from southern sympathizers in camp who named the place after the

Top: Despite numerous fires, many buildings in Warren are more than one hundred years old.

Middle: The Spotted Owl Shoot is the big annual event for the town of Warren.

Bottom: The Winter Inn is the only retail business in town.

Confederate capital. With a great deal of tension in the air, the Unionist miners left the camp and moved about a mile downstream. Here, they established a camp named Washington. As it turned out, Richmond was located on good placer ground. So, in 1866, the buildings were moved to Washington, and the ground was mined. The place boomed, and the population numbered in the thousands. In 1868, two stamp mills were built to crush ore here. In 1869, Washington became the county seat for Idaho County, winning over the honors from declining Florence.

Chinese miners arrived in large numbers during the 1870s. A "Chinatown" grew, and at its peak the population was thirteen hundred. Most panned for gold, but some farmed in the area for a livelihood. In what became known as the "Tong Wars," Chinese street gangs fought each other for control of Chinatowns, and some of this spilled over into Warren.

In 1875, Washington lost the honor of being the county seat to Mount Idaho. At about that time the town's name changed to Warren. In 1900, a forest fire destroyed almost everything in Warren. Today only a few private cabins here predate 1901. Then, in 1904, most of the new business district burned down in a town fire. Other problems were a short mining season and a lack of water.

Quartz mining continued in the area sporadically until at least 1932. The next phase of mining here consisted of dredging operations. The Idaho Gold Dredging Company built an airstrip in 1931 that is still in use today. A steam dredge was operated from 1931 to 1942, and two electric dredges were used during 1934. World War II ended gold mining in Warren.

The best route into Warren is from McCall. The road is closed during the winter, and the town is kept supplied by planes equipped with landing skis. During the forest fire of 2007, Warren was completely cut off, and the grass-strip airfield was their lifeline to the outside world. Even the telephone line installed during November 1995 was cut. Citizens refused to surrender to the fire and stayed in their town

A water cannon for hydraulic mining.

to fight it. Some structures on the edge of town were lost, but the town was saved.

Warren has a fair number of structures dating from 1901 to 1930. Pamphlets and signs provide information for those taking its walking tour. There is a café in town, the Winter Inn. There is no electricity here, so the Inn runs its own generator. The community has a small year-round population that balloons during the summer season. Warren is famous statewide for its Fourth of July celebration known as the "Spotted Owl Shoot," when the town is packed full of people. Don't worry; they don't shoot any owls.

YELLOW PINE (Valley)

This town was established around 1914. Its name came from the numerous ponderosa pines that surround the site. It served as a service center for the mining and timber industry. Yellow Pine is the jumping-off point for Big Creek, Stibnite, and the Thunder Mountain area. This is not a true ghost town but a sleepy seasonal tourist spot and nice stop. On my first visit, six of seven businesses were closed for the day. It was a nice spring day, and most owners had decided to close and go fishing; a note at the town store stated so. It also gave a phone number to call in case the accidental tourist, such as I, came by. I made the call and in ten minutes had service with a smile along with a free local history lesson.

Right: This row of cottages was company housing at Stibnite. They were moved by truck to Yellow Pine and are for sale.

Bottom: Downtown Yellow Pine.

Today the town is much smaller and quieter than in its boom days. A good number of tiny former company homes from Stibnite are lined up in neat rows and marked "For Sale." There are numerous old and historic buildings in this small hamlet. Some of the structures in use here today had been moved from abandoned mining towns in the area.

There are several roads into Yellow Pine. The best route in is from Cascade. If you want to drive to Big Creek, Stibnite, or Roosevelt, you have to pass through Yellow Pine.

GRAIN-SILO GHOSTS

While traveling the back roads of Idaho, I came across a small number of abandoned twentieth-century agricultural/railroad hamlets. It showed that not all ghost towns were mining centers. It also showed the economic risk of a community relying on one single industry.

The growth of the interstate highway system and accompanying trucking industry has cut deeply into the business trade of American railroads. Thousands of stops, depots, and miles of track have disappeared over the last half century. Many towns built to be next to railroads and their trade have been bypassed by the newer roads, so when the train traffic dries up, so does the town.

Top: The historic Yellow Pine School.
Bottom: All businesses along the highway are abandoned.

Another cause for the demise of these grain-silo communities is increased farm mechanization. It simply takes fewer workers to grow an acre of wheat. Fewer workers mean fewer paychecks and less spendable income in the town. Soon, what few businesses remain close or move to a bigger town, usually somewhere on the highway.

CORRAL (Camas)

Resting on the shoulders of Highway 20 is a sleepy little spot named Corral. This was a small railroad town that served the farming community. Today the grain silos are empty and the tracks are gone, sold off for scrap.

Above: The tracks are gone, but it is still easy to see where the railroad was.

Right: Sunday services are no longer held here.

While some houses were vacant, most were occupied. The old railroad bed and three abandoned grain elevators were plain to see. Scattered around this were a couple of busted businesses and an empty little church. State Highway 20 splits the town, with the larger portion sitting on the north side of the road.

Corral was a farm community on the Camas Prairie even before the Union Pacific built a railroad spur through here. The railroad would have been attracted to the water of Corral Creek for use in its steam locomotives. Water, as always, is precious in the West.

The name Corral comes from the early settlers who noticed the numerous natural corrals in the area.

Corral is located on State Highway 20 between Fairfield (the county seat) and Hill City, another grain silo ghost town.

DRUMMOND (Fremont)

This is a semi-ghost with a quiet population of thirteen. The town was founded in 1900. On my first visit, the local dog population (mostly friendly) seemed to outnumber the human population. A number of dogs came out in the street to introduce themselves with wagging tails.

Modern mechanization led to the loss of farm jobs, and government regulations led to the almost complete extinction of timber industry jobs in this area.

The railroad ended operations on this line in the mid-1980s. The tracks and ties have been removed and sold for scrap. The old railroad bed is still plainly visible.

A good portion of the field research for this section was conducted at Bob's Village Bar, the only business in town. I was greeted at the door by another vigorously wagging tail. The man who owned and ran the bar said he was the mayor of Drummond. He was kind enough to let a complete stranger barrage him with questions.

Above: This house belonged to one of the town's past mayors.

Left: False-front buildings are a common sight in Western ghost towns.

Being mountain prairie, this place is subject to the occasional breeze. On my first visit here, it came gently out of the west at a consistent 45 mph. The power lines overhead were humming like the strings of a harp.

Drummond is on Highway 32 and is shown on the state highway map.

HILL CITY (Camas)
ALTITUDE 5,098 FEET

Hill City is an unincorporated small collection of ranch and farmhouses split by Highway 20. It used to be much more. Mr. Nicklewaite picked the location as a town site when he learned that the railroad was being built through there. In the end, the railroad terminated here. It was a Union Pacific spur line and tied into another spur that serviced the mines north of Bellevue.

The town had a school, post office, and a business main street. There was a wooden grain elevator early on. After WWII, two larger concrete grain elevator complexes were built. The railroad spur served the grain elevators. All three grain elevators are still there today.

The town's first name was Prairie since it was located on the Camas Prairie. Prairie was a very common name, so it was probably rejected on the application for a post office. Then, the town's name was changed to Hill City. Its second name came from the Bennett Mountain Hills, which are just north of town. On my last visit to Hill City, the Bennett Mountain Hills were on fire—one of the many forest fires that plagued Idaho during summer 2007.

There is a cemetery a half mile north of town. The oldest grave here is dated 1915.

Middle: Two of the three grain elevators and the railroad bed at Hill City. This frame structure was the oldest of the grain elevators in Hill City.

Bottom: What's left of the Hill City business district.

Above: The third grain elevator.

The post office opened in 1912 and stayed in operation until ca. 2000. The post office is still visible inside a vacant store. An empty cash register and display case litter the building. The town had a school, which has been rebuilt and converted into a storage building. There is a second abandoned business building and the old railroad bed. The tracks have been ripped up and sold for scrap.

Hill City is fourteen miles southwest of Fairfield and is marked on the state highway map.

LAMONT (Teton)

This is a small, intact twentieth-century ghost town with no population. There is a grain silo and an old railroad bed from when this was a small agriculture center. The railroad was a Union Pacific spur line that ended at Marysville.

When the railroad shut down the line, it put the grain silo out of business. No train, no silo, no town. Later, even the tracks were ripped up.

Lamont is bisected by State Highway 32. It can be found on a state road atlas and on old maps, but it is not shown on the current official state highway map. Another grain silo ghost town, Drummond, is just up the highway. They shared the same rail spur and a lot of the same history.

Left: The grain silo at Lamont.

Right: Some of the buildings in this town date to its earliest days.

Bottom: A few business structures are across the road from the grain elevator.

Without its gold and silver, the Owyhee Mountains would never have received much attention from development.

OWYHEE MOUNTAINS

The Owyhee Mountains are low-set desert mountains, rough, rock-studded, scrub-strewn, and desolate. Things that are common here: rocks, sagebrush, and rattlesnakes. Things that are rare: good roads, shade, and water. This is a place where you have a choice: you can die of sunstroke in the day or freeze to death later that night. The heat in the summer is brutal, and even though it's desert, the place gets buried in snow during the winter.

From the very beginning, hostile Indians were a hair-raising problem for miners or trappers in the Owyhee Mountains. The name "Owyhee" comes from an attempt by the Hudson Bay Company to spell "Hawaii." They were doing so in honor of two of their "former" employees who had come from the Hawaiian Islands. Indians had killed them on what has become the Owyhee River, and the mountains get their name from them. This isn't what the place is famous for; what brought fame here were hordes of fortune-seekers looking for El Dorado.

It started when a thirty-man prospecting party from Placerville discovered the Owyhee Basin gold placers. The group was led by Michael Jordan and was supposedly looking for either the Lost Blue Bucket Mine or the legendary Sinker Creek.

These are two western legends that a couple of states claim as their own. They both involve 1840s wagon trains. The story of the Lost Blue Bucket Mine, or at least one version, begins with an Indian attack on an Oregon-bound 1845 wagon train. For protection, some of the wagon train party took shelter in what turned out to be a mine tunnel. Near the entrance was an old blue bucket containing some rocks. A few curious children picked up the rocks and started playing with them. They examined them and tossed them at each other. A few took some of the interesting rocks and put them in their pockets. It was only weeks later on the trail that a closer examination revealed the rocks contained gold. By then, nobody could remember the mine's location.

The story of Sinker Creek is another tale of treasure found, then lost. It involves another western-bound wagon train. While fishing for dinner in a stream one evening, the men discovered some soft rocks that could be hammered onto their fishing lines to be used as sinkers. Upon reaching the gold fields of California, these pioneers discovered that their soft rocks were gold nuggets. Once again, no one could remember where they found the gold.

The Jordan party found neither the legendary Sinker Creek nor the Lost Blue Bucket Mine, but they did find placer gold in the Owyhee Mountain Basin streams, and that was good enough for them.

The discovery of the gold placers led to an immediate rush, but the deposits were thin and soon played out. During this stampede, large deposits of lode silver were discovered, and a second and bigger rush was soon on. It was this second rush that produced most of the mining and most of the towns of the Owyhee Mountains.

This was the assay office.

To reach the ghost towns in these mountains, it is best to approach from the Jordan Valley in Oregon. The roads from Murphy or Reynolds in Idaho are too rough. Just another example of "You can't get there from here" that one experiences traveling in Idaho.

DE LAMAR (Owyhee)

De Lamar started as a true boomtown. A sailing ship captain and Colorado developer by the name of Joseph R. De Lamar decided to trade his life on the waves for a more solid and hopefully more lucrative one of mining on the land.

It started in September 1886, when Mr. De Lamar bought the mining interest of the Wagontown property of John A. Wilson. Wagontown was a small settlement with a couple of silver mines and a mill. Nothing remains of it today. After improving the operation of the Wagontown mill and his mine there, Mr. De Lamar decided to expand his mining business. He continued to buy up mining claims and in 1888, founded his own town, De Lamar.

De Lamar was just two miles up Jordan Creek from Wagontown. He also owned a mine called the Wilson, on the hill overlooking his new town. For the mine he built a mill, a tramway down the mountain to the mill, a machine workshop, assay office, blacksmith shop, a two-story boardinghouse, large ore bins, a superintendent's house, and a mine office. For the town he built a two-and-a-half-story hotel, a large two-story schoolhouse, stores, cabins, a red light district, and other facilities. The town also had a church. A newspaper, the *De Lamar Nugget*, was first published on May 5, 1891. Mr. De Lamar sold the mine in 1891 for a good profit to an English company.

Most of the community lay within the narrow Jordan Creek Valley, exposing it to flood. It was (and is) prone to brush fires in the summer and blizzards in the winter.

Because of a spike in precious metal prices, the mine here has been reopened on a small scale. This new mine is an open pit operation

Top: The house is older than the trees that shade it.

Bottom: Old houses are stretched out for miles along Jordan Creek.

and digging for gold and silver ores. A closed and posted gate kept me from visiting this portion of the site. What part of the old mining operation the new one has consumed, I could not say. Of the often-photographed assay office and boardinghouse, I found only the former. Photographs dated from 2001 showed the boardinghouse still standing and next to the assay office. On my visit, I didn't even see its collapsed remains, and it was a rather large building. Other remains, mostly second generation, run through the creek valley for a couple miles. These include the almost unrecognizable remains of the mill.

DEWEY (Owyhee)

Located just downstream of Silver City on Jordan Creek are the remains of a silver mining town called Dewey. The place was first called Booneville. It serviced the local gold and silver mines. During 1896, the place became a true boomtown. A miner calling himself Colonel Dewey bought a mine and most of Booneville, then proceeded to put a lot of money into both. A three-story hotel and a post office were built. The hotel was a large frame and rather grand structure with a three-story front porch running the length of the building. A new twenty-stamp mill ensured the mining operation was not a quiet one. After having done all this, W. H. Dewey felt justified to change the name of the town to Dewey.

The town received electricity in 1901. After that, it received bad news. First, the Boise, Nampa and Owyhee Railroad decided not to build an anticipated railroad terminus in Dewey. Then the hotel burned down. Next, most of the mines closed, followed finally by the post office.

Remains today are a few foundations, the concrete shell of a power plant, and the hillside terraces of a mill. If you take the road from Oregon to Silver City, Dewey is along the way and cannot be missed.

SILVER CITY (Owyhee)
ALTITUDE 6,300 FEET

This is probably Idaho's best known and most-written-about ghost town. Located in the heart of the Owyhee Mountains, it was considered isolated even during its boom period.

Top: These are the remains of the mill and the concrete shell of the powerhouse.

Bottom: These are the foundations of buildings that used to sit in front of the Grand Dewey Hotel.

Left top: The church has a commanding view of the town, especially the red light district.

Left bottom: This was the Stoddard Mansion.

Right top: The Idaho Hotel has a restaurant and a few alleged spirits.

Silver City was founded in December 1863. From its beginning, the town competed with neighboring Ruby City for everything. In the short run, Silver City won everything. In just a little more than two years, Ruby City succumbed to its upstart neighbor. Even most of its buildings were moved to Silver City. A few, including the famous Idaho Hotel, still stand today. In 1865, a rich silver lode was found on War Eagle Mountain overlooking the town. This was a huge boon to most of the surrounding communities. By 1866, Silver City won the county seat of Owyhee County from Ruby City.

Top: A two-story outhouse. The reason for it was extremely deep winter snows.

Bottom: This vault shows where a bank once stood.

Right: This souvenir shop is the only other retail business in Silver City. It's also a good place for local information.

At its peak, Silver City had a population of about twenty-five hundred, its own newspaper, the *Owyhee Avalanche*, and the first telegraphic wire in the territory. There were more than three hundred homes and seventy-five businesses. The list of businesses included six general stores, two lumberyards, three barbershops, saloons, brothels, drugstores, doctors, lawyers, a tailor shop, a photography studio, an undertaker, a hospital, and two hotels. The community also enjoyed churches, an Odd Fellows Hall, and a Masonic Lodge. There was even a small "Chinatown" and a Chinese cemetery. The town had telephones by 1880 and electricity by 1890.

Silver City had two "Indian scares" in its lifetime. The first was during summer 1864. The situation got so tense that the citizens barricaded part of the town and organized a company of volunteers. Fortunately, hostilities were ended, but only by forcing the Indians onto a reservation. In 1878, a serious uprising led by Chief Buffalo Horn was directed against Silver City. The settlers and miners were tipped off about the Indian attack plan, and they organized another company of volunteers. They decided to attack the Indians before they reached the town. Instead, they got ambushed by the Indians and were forced to retreat. During the fight, Chief Buffalo Horn was

killed. Dispirited, the other Indians rode off to Oregon, and Silver City was saved.

When they weren't exchanging gunfire with local Indians, the settlers here were quite busy shooting each other. There was a lot of violence in Silver City, which is borne out by the cemeteries and old newspaper articles. Mine owners fought with the miners and with each other.

Sometimes, professional gunslingers were hired to do the job. Both crime and drunkenness were common on the streets of this city. Another problem bred by the living conditions here were epidemics. In many ways, this silver rush was the Wild West at its worst; on the other hand, it was one of the few rushes to show a profit. The ore in the Owyhee was high grade, and there was a lot of it. Millions of dollars worth of silver and lead were taken out of the ground. Silver City had the longest run of all the Owyhee Mountain mine towns.

One more small boost came to the town during WWI and its higher metal prices. Eventually, even here, the boom sputtered to a stop. The ore veins pinched out or ran too deep. In 1935, Silver City lost the county seat to Murphy. By 1940, Silver City had become a virtual ghost town. The last retail businesses closed in 1942. Around then, electricity to the town was shut off. The lights had truly gone out in Silver City. Today it has had a small rebirth as a tourist spot. Silver City has to be one of the best ghost towns of the American West. The dozens of weather-beaten buildings set against the backdrop of the desert mountains make this a photographer's paradise.

Even though only one in eight structures remain from the town's glory days, this leaves seventy buildings still standing. The ruins of many more lie about. These consist of chimneys, foundations, bank vaults, piles of lumber, or other such items that point to where hundreds more buildings were. Many buildings are being restored to their original conditions. Keep in mind that most are more than 140 years old. A partial list of some of Silver City's fabulous buildings are

One of two powder magazines you see on your drive to Silver City. The town folk had the good sense to build these stone bunkers outside town.

the Catholic church, the school, the Masonic Hall, the I.O.O.F. Hall, the Stoddard Mansion, the two-story outhouses, and much, much more. Each one has its own story, its own history.

The best is the Idaho Hotel. It was moved from Ruby City to Silver City in 1866. It is allegedly haunted and has been the subject of television specials. It is open for business, and the current owner does not like ghost hunters. They scare his customers more than any suspected spook. There is no electricity, so guests are given old-time lanterns, which, of course, just adds to the place's allure. This is also the only restaurant in town. Across the street is the town's only other business, Pat's Gift Shop. The owners of both are very friendly and kindly consented to let me interview them. The whole place is a ghost town hunter's dream. If Hollywood has the need of an authentic western movie set, this is it.

May to October is the season for the town. The summer population is a dozen or more, but during the winter it drops to just one. Winter can produce four to six feet of snow in the Owyhee Mountains and close all routes to the area. Roads to Silver City are rough. On my first three attempts to reach the town, I was turned back by roads closed to flood damage or brush fires. The best way to Silver City is from the Jordan Valley in Oregon. The roads from Murphy or Reynolds in Idaho to the east are much tougher routes to take. One more example of "You can't get there from here" in Idaho. Silver City is easy to locate; it's shown on the state highway map.

The Masonic Lodge has been fully restored.

OTHER OWYHEE GHOST TOWNS

There are a few ghost town sites in the Owyhee Mountains I did not visit, and I recommend that most of you shouldn't even try. There is a list of reasons why. To start with, the environment in general is hostile—hot days, cold nights, and no shade or water but plenty of sun and rattlesnakes. This is not a place to break down, get lost, hurt, or travel alone. The road system here is a maze of mostly bad

The back roads of the Owyhee Mountains are not a place to break down.

dirt mountain roads. The place could be the next film location for the "Survivor" television program. If you are not from here, you need a local guide, a GPS, or a good set of topo maps with compass and the ability to use them.

Also, in most cases there are few or no original remains worth seeing. Last but not least, the majority of the sites are on private property, so do not trespass. All these locations are in Owyhee County and the mountains.

FAIRVIEW

This town had more than one hundred buildings at its peak. It served the needs of the miners on War Eagle Mountain. There was a post office in use here from September 27, 1872, to September

13, 1878. A miners' union cemetery was started during 1873 and used until 1886. A fire destroyed most of Fairview in October 1875. Remains here are a few mineshafts, the foundation of a mill, some collapsed structures, and a weather-beaten cemetery with most of its graves unmarked. The road leading here is a four-wheel drive.

FLINT

Flint is ten to thirteen miles southwest of Silver City. The route here is a rough mountain dirt road. The town site is on private property. A cemetery is across a creek and up a hill to the southwest of the town. Two isolated graves rest on another hilltop—the graves of William L. Black and his daughter-in-law, Emma Myers. The two were killed in an Indian attack. The town lost several other citizens to such attacks. The U.S. Cavalry was finally called in to "put down" the Indians. Several sources say there are a mill, several frame houses, and a couple of other buildings still standing, but these sources are dated and the data suspect.

When Flint was booming, it had fifteen hundred inhabitants, two mills, a post office, livery stable, stage station, stores, and saloons.

RUBY CITY

This was the second town to pop up from the Owyhee Mountains gold/silver rush. The first was Boonville, but its location was pinched between steep hills, so a more spacious town site was needed. Ruby City was laid out farther up Jordan Creek. This was during late summer 1863. Silver City popped up just a mile away in December 1863. The two towns immediately became competitors.

On December 31, 1864, Ruby City became the seat of Owyhee County. The town had one thousand people and the district's first newspaper, the *Owyhee Avalanche*. The newspaper first printed on August 19, 1865, lasted only one year, then moved to Silver City. The town lasted only a little longer.

Ruby City was constantly swept by the winds and was farther from the mines than Silver City. Businesses and people started moving there for the better location, and at the beginning of 1867, so did the county seat. Even most of the better buildings were moved to Silver City. The town quickly faded. The howling of hundreds of miners drinking in saloons was replaced with that of the lone coyote and the wind.

For a while, the cemetery was still used. The last recorded burial was on October 15, 1881. In an unusual note, the body was delivered to the cemetery alive. Henry McDonald had been convicted and sentenced to death in Silver City. He was held in the jail there until the day of his execution, then taken by wagon to the old Ruby City cemetery. There a scaffold had been built and his grave already dug—a chilling sight for the condemned to behold. To further set the somber mood, a storm raged overhead. Despite the storm, three hundred people showed up to witness his execution. Silver City had a cemetery, with gamblers, drunks, gunmen, and even Chinese buried in it. Of course, all these people had their own sections; still, they could share the same graveyard, but not Henry McDonald. That makes this "recycled cemetery" a true "boot hill."

The only remains at the old town site are the old weather-beaten cemetery. If you want to see more of Ruby City, go to Silver City. Some of its buildings are still standing or lying on the ground there.

SOUTH MOUNTAIN CITY

Another early mining camp of Owyhee County was Bullion City. The city was laid out in the early 1870s. When the townspeople applied for a post office, they had a common problem: it was too common of a name. Their application was rejected, so they changed the name to South Mountain City. In 1874, the South Mountain Consolidated Mining Company built a smelting furnace to process the lead and silver ore from the area's mines. The major mines here were the Bay State, the Black Giant, the Crown Point, and the Golconda. For several years, it was the only smelter in Idaho.

Mining resumed here in the 1950s, and it consumed most, if not all of the original remains. The slagheap from the boom days has probably been reworked, and I doubt if it even remains. This site is southwest of Silver City and twenty miles southeast of Jordan Valley, Oregon. It is deep in the mountains among bad roads and on private property.

TRIANGLE

Triangle was a town that serviced ranchers in the Southern Owyhee Mountains. It started around the time of the first mining boom and lasted well into the late twentieth century. It had been marked on state highway maps, but recently the site has been removed. The town location was the southernmost of all towns in the Owyhee Mountains and is isolated by any standard. The roads to it are rough, even in good weather.

In its history, the town had a post office, and the local ranchers had trouble with hostile Indians. The town's name comes from the Triangle Ranch. It was the biggest ranch in the area and is famous in its own right. A book has even been written about the ranch. Today, the town of Triangle is on private property. A local ranch bought the site. Maps show an airstrip at this location.

SALMON AREA GHOST TOWNS

Centrally located in the state, this area is large and varied. Mining still goes on here. It was home to some of the state's first gold rushes. Today, it is the tourists who stampede here in the summer who provide most of the gold. They come to camp, fish, hike, hunt, climb, ride, and ghost town hunt. Another important industry here is timber. Be careful of both mining and logging trucks on the narrow roads in the area. Numerous large forest fires caused much damage over the whole area during summer 2007. It caused me more than a little trouble in some remote areas. The danger of being cut off was high. Smoke shows in some of my photos.

For the purposes of this book, I have enlarged what many would consider the Salmon area. The town of Salmon itself is a nice stop

Idaho's backcountry roads must traverse rugged and mountainous terrain. The haze in the photo is due to a forest fire in the area.

and makes for a great center base for operations while visiting numerous old ghost towns of the area. There are plenty of hotels, restaurants, stores, and a history museum. There is a park in the center of town. Many enjoy swimming in the Salmon River there.

COBALT (Lemhi)

Cobalt is a town named after the metal that was mined there. The ore came from the Blackbird Mine. The first ore to be discovered near the Blackbird Mine was copper. A Lemhi prospector named Indian Tom found it in summer 1892. Gold and nickel were discovered in 1893 and cobalt in 1901. In the 1960s and 1970s, Cobalt probably was Idaho's best ghost town. At the time, it had more than one hundred buildings standing in mint condition. For decades, the abandoned town was kept on the state highway map; more recently, it has been removed.

Work at the Blackbird Mine started in summer 1895. A small log cabin town sprang up next to the mine and mill. Like the mine and mill, its name was Blackbird. Gold and copper were both mined here. By 1896, things looked promising, and major development started.

The buildings have been disappearing from Cobalt's old Main Street.

Many houses still try to hide among the trees.

Mining continued at Blackbird, except for a four-year break for World War I, until 1921. Then the place became a ghost town of log cabins. Some of these structures were here until at least the 1970s.

In 1939, the mine reopened with a government contract for cobalt. This was a large, modern development that was to have a company town. The first location of the town was next to the mine, six miles from the present location. The valley was too narrow for both the new town and mine operation, so the town was moved to its present location and still called Blackbird. Nothing remains of the first town location. It was a real boom. A large town was built quickly, and it was a busy place through 1959. The school had eight grades with 120 students. The mine had 450 employees, and the town's population was 2,000. At first, this location was also called Blackbird, but later the name was changed to Cobalt. When the government contract expired in 1959, both the mine and the town shut down. There had been small spurts of mining activity at the Blackbird in 1963 and 1967 and from 1980 to 1984.

This gate station was one of many services in the company town.

As a company town, it had almost everything. There was a fire station, grocery store, recreation hall, and post office, and by its nature, it also had a real uniform look about it. Most of the buildings were constructed with white asbestos siding.

When the town became a ghost in 1960, it was padlocked and given a caretaker. For years, the town sat dormant, waiting to reopen with the mine. It never happened. After a good number of years, everybody gave up the ghost, and buildings from Cobalt were sold and relocated to other towns. I have been watching the town disappear over the last decade. Today, there are only about a dozen structures left.

Cobalt is located on Panther Creek Road in the heart of the Salmon–Challis National Forest. The location is marked on old state highway maps, the current state road atlas, and the area National Forest map. The valley that it lies in is beautiful and easy to access off Highway 93. Currently, there is a small village here that unofficially goes by the name of Panther Creek. It has a small county saloon/café. The old Cobalt town site is just up the road from the saloon. Caution: If you visit the old mine site, be aware that the mining operation has contaminated Blackbird Creek with heavy metals. Do not drink the water.

FORNEY (Lemhi)

Forney started as a gold placer camp before 1890. One Mr. Forney, who was a prospector and trapper, discovered gold dust in Porphyry Creek. Despite his good fortune, Forney soon left, but his name stayed. The placer deposits quickly played out, but Forney not only hung on, it thrived. Placer tin was also found here, but not enough to mine. The town prospered as a small service center for area loggers, miners, ranchers, and travelers between 1890 and 1948. Sawmill Gulch is very close to the town, and at one time it had a sawmill in it. A school was built in Forney in 1909. In 1910, the census reported a population of 150 here. There were stores, a livery stable, and the Fourth of July Hotel.

The first post office in Forney was opened in 1890, and its postmaster was E. P. Trealor. Forage and feed were stored at Forney for horses hauling supplies to and ore from, the area mines. There was a saloon, of course, and the owner kept a cougar as a pet. In fact, while researching the history of the town, I found at least five photos of town residents posing with their pet cougars!

The town thrived until 1948, and then it just faded away. Telephone service was discontinued in the 1940s, when the National Forest Service discontinued maintenance of the lines for budget and jurisdictional reasons. The school closed in 1948. A country gas station-and-food store combination lasted here until the 1960s.

The remains of Forney can be found on Panther Creek Road, south of Cobalt, where Porphyry Creek enters Panther Creek. The location is easy to find and is marked on the National Forest map of the area. It is at the intersection of Panther Creek Road and Yellowjacket Road. Both are National Forest roads, with the latter giving you

Top: A few old log cabins still stand at Forney.

Middle: A structure from Forney's more modern times. The road to the right leads to Yellow Jacket.

Bottom: These concrete steps once led to a substantial structure one source said was a school, but I was not able to confirm this.

Top: A two-section outhouse. Each section had two seats. The citizens of Forney must have been very personable.

Bottom: This large structure served as a store and, at another time, the town's post office.

a rough route to the ghost town of Yellowjacket. There are few standing structures left in Forney, although most of what is left are original buildings, many being outhouses.

Just south of here on the same road is the tiny ghost town of Merritt. Both ghost towns were sites I stumbled upon during my travels.

GILMORE (Lemhi)

Gilmore was a hard rock, lead-silver, and gold mining operation in the Lemhi Mountain Range. Gold was discovered in 1873 here, but initially not in commercial quantities. Then in 1879, quantities of silver and lead were found in the area, and by 1880 a mining district was organized. Ralph Nichols, area pioneer and mine developer, started a mining camp near one of the large lead-silver veins.

In fact, a great deal of ore had been discovered in the Lemhi Mountain Range—the trouble was mining, milling, and moving it. All this required substantial capital investment. The money and the machinery started to arrive in 1882. First, a thirty-ton smelter was

Most of the housing at Gilmore is older than the boom-period business structures.

installed on Spring Mountain at the town of Hahn. In fall 1885, a two-stack smelter was built across the valley at Nicholia. Due to fuel shortages and other problems, these smelters could not run all the time. In between operations, ore was hauled by wagon out of the valley to railheads.

From here it was shipped to Omaha or Kansas City for processing. In 1888, a drop in lead prices, a worker's strike, and a mine fire put a temporary halt to operations. Operations were restarted, but in 1890 the Nicholia smelter shut down. For the next four years, ore was hauled out by wagon with horse teams or steam tractors. The wagons soon wore out, and transportation made operations at Gilmore unprofitable. Once again, the community slipped into an economic depression. Not until 1910 would things fiscally change.

That year, the Gilmore and Pittsburgh Railroad was completed in the valley and started hauling ore out. It was an immediate boon for Gilmore. The town grew to a stable population of six hundred. Mining operations at Gilmore were steady until after 1919. The post–World War I financial collapse led to restricted operations until 1924. After that, an increase in metal prices helped spur mining activity again.

Gilmore was named after a pioneer, John T. Gilmer. He was one of the partners of the Gilmer and Salisbury Stage Company. The town, in fact, had been called Gilmer, but in 1903, when a post office was established, the name changed to Gilmore. This is because the U.S. Postal Service in Washington, D.C., had misspelled the name.

At one time, the town had seven saloons, three stores, two hotels, two dance halls, a theater, two trucking companies, a two-room schoolhouse, a bank, a post office, and a power plant. In 1929, the combination of a power plant explosion and the stock market crash doomed Gilmore. The town emptied quickly.

A livery stable and old housing dot the hillside.

Numerous mine cabins and structures hide among the pines on the mountain above Gilmore.

Gilmore is south of Leadore on Highway 28. Almost half of the buildings in Leadore are vacant and interesting to photograph. Still, the town is not a ghost but can provide you with food and gas while you tour the area.

Remains of the Gilmore town site are scattered over a large area on the side of a mountain. The town site rests among sagebrush with a backdrop of pine trees covering the mountain. Numerous mines and buildings are hidden under the trees. The old railroad bed snakes across the desert to the town site. Buildings in town include log construction from earlier phases and well-constructed businesses from the 1910 boom. Many buildings show signs of multiple occupancies. Vandals have been a severe problem to the site. Sadly, in recent times, they burned down a rather large two-story hotel.

Two rather unique things about this ghost town—first, it has an adjacent National Forest campground, Silver Lake; second, parts of the town are for sale. Caution: the road to the campground is very narrow and steep.

HAHN (Lemhi)

On a desert hillside seven miles southeast of Gilmore is the old town site of Hahn. It was named for a man from Missouri who built the smelter. There, at its height of activity in 1884, the town's population reached only one hundred. A thirty-ton smelter was built at Spring Mountain in 1882, and it ran through the mid-1880s. The Spring Mountain Mining Company built the smelter, an office, a boardinghouse, and ore bins at Hahn.

Hahn served as a community center and had a post office for the numerous mines on Spring Mountain. The post office was open from 1909 to 1911. Another thirty-ton smelter was built at this site in 1909. This smelter ran only a short time during 1909 and 1910. One mine still visible today was actually in town. Mining was for lead and silver.

The most significant thing here today is the historical marker. This place is more an archeological site than it is a ghost town. Occasionally, you can see the outline of a rock foundation or a raised mound of earth where a building used to be. The dry creek that descended the mountains here had half a dozen small but breached dams in it. Dry conditions caused water shortage problems in this valley. Alongside the dry creek and running parallel to the National Forest road were the remains of an old wagon road. There was supposed to be a cemetery, a slagheap, and concrete foundations, but I did not locate any.

The Hahn town site is located seven miles south of Gilmore. Take Highway 28 to National Forest Road 296, aka Spring Mountain Canyon Road. There is a sign, so the turnoff is easy to find. The National Forest road is short but rough; proceed slowly.

Top: The turnoff to Hahn is well marked and easy to find.

Bottom: Not much remains of Hahn, so if you go, do it for the scenery.

KINGVILLE (Lemhi)

Across the Lemhi Valley from the mining town of Nicholia was the small community of Kingville. Kingville used sixteen beehive kilns to make charcoal for the smelter at Nicholia. The reason for the kilns to be located across the valley is simple: that's where the wood was. Wagons would haul in green timber for the kilns, then haul out charcoal for the smelter. This was hard, hot, heavy labor, and it covered the town with smoke and dust.

This was a small town of about one hundred. It was started in the early 1880s and went bust in 1890 when the Viola Mine in Nicholia shut down. Mail came from the town of Hahn, and children went to school at Nicholia. Construction consisted of log cabins. The town site burned down, and all that remains are four of the kilns. There is a historical marker that assists you with a self-guided tour.

LEESBURG (Lemhi)

During summer 1866, five miners from Montana—Frank Sharkey, Bill Smith, Lige (Elijah) Mulkey, Ward Girton, and Joe Rapp—had grown tired of working for wages and headed to the Salmon River to do gold prospecting. They found their El Dorado on July 16, 1866 (National Forest Service brochures put the date at July 18), when the party found rich placer deposits in the Napias Creek near the mouth of Wards Gulch.

By August, the rush was on, and it would be frantic. Sources claim that at its peak, there were one hundred businesses and four thousand people in Leesburg and seven thousand in the Basin. The rush to Leesburg helped open the floodgate of mining development in Central Idaho in the last third of the nineteenth century. For the first few months, it was a growing tent camp. By early winter, a construction boom was underway, even though most people had left with the first snow. The camp was full of southern veterans of the Civil War. They named the camp after General Robert E. Lee, their hero, and called it Leesburg.

Main Street of Leesburg.

Veterans of the Union Army objected but were well outnumbered, so they moved next door. They called their settlement Grantsville. At the height of the first boom, there were more than one hundred businesses and as many as three thousand people in the combined town and maybe seven thousand in the Basin. The community thrived through 1869. After the boom, the town's population shrunk to a few hundred and stayed that way through the 1920s. Winters were harsh here, and the heavy snows caused numerous supply problems almost every season.

Like a lot of Idaho pioneer mining towns, Leesburg had a Chinatown and a Chinese boom or phase. Starting in 1870, Chinese miners showed up to rework claims abandoned by white miners. They lived in their own community called "Chinatown." They also had their own cemetery, but when they left, they dug up the bodies for reburial in China. One remaining cabin has a Chinese inscription.

I found this and a few other structures off Main Street in the woods.

The cemetery at Leesburg is in rough condition.

The Leesburg Stage, using a Concord Coach, ran from the mid-1890s to at least 1928. What is left of Leesburg are the remains of more than a dozen log buildings that lined Main Street. Two of the structures on the east end of the site are what is left of Grantsville. These structures were built anywhere from the 1870s to the 1930s. There is another building and an outhouse in the woods on the Leesburg, or west, side. I think it is on property belonging to the mining company. Tailings can be seen for miles down Napias Creek, the aftereffects of hydraulic and dredge mining in the area. The hydraulic mining started about 1930, and the dredging was done during 1941–42.

There is a cemetery just south of town. It contains at least seventeen graves and is in rough shape. There are two ways into Leesburg; the southern route is the best one. The road has been greatly improved due to a new gold mining operation next to it. The old town site is protected. It is 32.7 road miles from Salmon. Have a good map before attempting this or any other backcountry drive.

Top: May's business district.

Bottom: May had numerous cafés, halls, and lodges.

MAY (Lemhi)

May is a ranching town that has seen much busier days. It became the area's cattle and sheep rancher's town when the post office opened during 1897. The first postmaster was Rudolph Wright. The town was named after his wife, May.

The town had a hotel, dancehall, school, post office, an I.O.O.F. hall, a National Grange Society Hall, several saloons, restaurants, and more. The Grange Hall sometimes doubled as a roller-skating rink. Today, all but one of the town's businesses is history, and the school has been consolidated with the one in Patterson. A number of abandoned buildings date from the early 1900s. A second Grange Hall built here is still in use. May's location is shown on the state highway map. There is a small population here.

Top: A 1930s-era gas pump and station stand next to an even older building.

Bottom: This was a hotel and nightclub.

MERRITT (Lemhi)

Located on Panther Creek Road, at the junction of Panther Creek and Fourth of July Creek, is a ramshackle collection of collapsed buildings with an interesting history. This site started as a homestead or mining claim by pioneer Milt Merritt.

With the mining boom, it grew into a small community. There was a post office here, and its first postmaster was Milt Merritt. He was succeeded by Mrs. Belle O'Conner. Mail was dropped off to be distributed to mines farther west in the mountains. There also was a sawmill. It would be used to provide timber for the same mines. Barbed wire, farm, and ranch equipment scattered about the place shows that after having been a town, the site was used for other purposes. Telephone poles adjacent to the old cabins indicate this site was occupied long after its pioneer days. This place is on private property with a seasonal cabin. Do not trespass. Please be respectful, and only view from the roadside. If you stop to take photos, pull over completely. Please be safe, and do not block the road.

This cluster of buildings had log walls, lumber for roofs, and utility poles.

A few cabins hide in the brush here.

A confession: I do not know the name of this small community; Merritt was just my best guess. This was one of several locations I just stumbled upon during my field research trip. The information about the site comes from the Salmon Museum, but they didn't know the name of the place either. Still, the museum was a big help in my research, and it makes a nice visit if you are in Salmon.

PATTERSON (Lemhi)

This is a wrecked tungsten-mining ghost town. It is located in the semi-arid Pahsimeroi Valley on the southern end of the Farm to Market Road. Panning for gold and silver started here in the early 1880s. Little was found, and ore veins that were discovered proved to be too low of grade.

Top: A gas station at left. I don't know what the steps belonged to; now you could only guess.

Middle: Most of what remains of Patterson looks like this.

Bottom: The gas pumps still work—that is, if the generator is running.

The story changed in 1903 when tungsten was discovered in Patterson Creek Canyon. Like most of Idaho at the time, it was remote and lacked proper transportation. Development took some time, and it was not until 1911 that production began. A mill was constructed here in 1912. Major additional development came during 1934. The most important and longest continuous-running mine here was the Ima. Mining activity continued until 1958; then the Ima shut down and most of the equipment was sold off. Tungsten or wolfram ore is still there, but the cost of extraction had become prohibitive. As usual, there are rumors of the mine being reopened.

The town of Patterson served the mines and its miners as well as local ranchers. The site is on Patterson Creek at the mouth of Patterson Canyon. The location is still shown on the state highway map. The town's name comes from John Patterson, who discovered a ledge of silver along the creek in 1879.

The road to Patterson is paved, but there are no services there and few in the entire valley. There is camping in the area, but most of the roads to any sites are rutted dirt when dry and worse when wet.

SHOUP (Lemhi)

This is a nice ghost town to visit for a whole lot of reasons, one being you can get a good malt here.

This town's history begins on April 24, 1862, when Ben Harrison discovered placer gold here in the Salmon River. The first year-round mining camp was established here in 1868. It took more than another decade before meaningful lode discoveries were made in 1881. At first, the community was named Boulder, but when its residents applied for a post office under that name, the postal service rejected it because the name was already in use in the territory. They reapplied under the name of Shoup in 1883, and it was accepted. The name came from George L. Shoup, one of the leading citizens of Lemhi County, who would later become governor of the state. Initially, supplies could reach the site only by use of pack mules

The remains of a mill at Shoup.

trekking over the mountains or rafts floating down the Salmon River. Eventually, a wagon road would partially ease supply problems.

The river valley here is steep and narrow, which confined development to a narrow ribbon of buildings up and downstream.

By 1888, the area had more than three hundred lode mines and, of course, even more miners. There were eight mines in town alone. More miners meant more business for Shoup. Besides the normal complement of saloons, the town also had an art gallery and an opera house. There were high hopes that the mining would attract a railroad, but the area's terrain ensured the development of any such dream would come with a large price tag.

During its height of glory, Shoup had a population more than six hundred and was situated on both banks of the Salmon River. Bridges connected the two halves. The bridges are now history. Today, fisherman, rafters, and tourists know Shoup. Just as you enter the town, there is a small yet interesting family-owned general store. It provides services for locals and outdoor enthusiasts. Whenever I stop in Shoup, I get a chocolate malt in the general store. The store also serves as the area post office, and if the generator is running, it's a gas station. They also rent cabins. The walls of the store are full of old black and white photos of the town. Behind the store, a good number of foundations cover the hillside. They show the outline of a mill, other buildings, and sidewalks. Old buildings or their remains line both sides of the river for about a mile. Drive slowly, or better yet, get out and walk. The road has numerous blind turns, and too often boulders, pedestrians, stopped traffic, or wildlife can appear out of nowhere on it.

Until recently, there was one gold mine in town still operating that also gave tours. Today the mine is shut down, and tours are only by special appointment. On my last visit, the kind mine owners allowed me to tag along on one of these tour groups.

Shoup is west of North Fork on a paved road. Its location is marked on the state highway map.

The "Old Hill Mine" is now closed except to special tours.

YELLOWJACKET (Lemhi)

Yellowjacket was a small, isolated gold mining town that had more ups and downs than a Coney Island roller coaster. In late summer 1869, Long "Doc" Wilson discovered placer gold on Yellowjacket Creek. This was followed by Nathan Smith leading a party of prospectors to the area. On their return, they told stories of finding another "Boise Basin." With this news, four hundred men took off from the Loon Creek digs and rushed toward Yellowjacket Creek. The stampede left on September 24 and almost depopulated the Loon Creek camps.

The strike turned out to be a hoax. There were very few placer deposits in Yellowjacket Creek. In fact, it was thought that someone had salted the first discovery. As luck would have it, these tricked prospectors still had the last laugh. While they were panning the creek, they discovered some major quartz leads that would prove to be productive. The joy of the second discovery was also short-lived. These prospectors were equipped to pan or mine only small pockets of gold.

Major development was needed, and once again there was the challenge of Idaho's rugged terrain and isolation of the site. It took until 1875 for a small three-stamp mill to be completed. In April 1883, a ten-stamp mill was packed in. Eventually, the mill would grow to a sixty-stamp that was water-powered. A sawmill was also packed in. The mule trains came all the way from Mackay, and even in June, snow was a common problem on the trails. In 1895 a wagon road from Challis was completed and reduced the town's transportation problem. Strikes were a problem in 1896. By 1900, things had slowed down. In 1910, a cyanide plant was installed. This operation lasted until 1914. Another revival came in 1922, and it was large enough that others invested money in the town, including building a new five-story hotel. In 1924, the mine shut down, and work on the hotel stopped before it was completed. A water giant was used in 1924 in an attempt at hydraulic mining, with disappointing results. Development work and lode mining resumed

Top: This hotel was open in 1924; it is now missing the roof and fifth floor.

Bottom: Rust shows that this equipment has been idle for decades.

The large Yellowjacket Mill has been stripped of most of its machinery.

in 1929 and continued on a small scale through 1938. Since then, there have been only small spurts of mining activity.

At its peak between 1890 and 1900, Yellowjacket's population ranged somewhere from 200 to 1,000. There were three saloons, at least two stores, a livery, a boardinghouse, two restaurants, and more providing services to the miners at the town's peak.

Although Yellowjacket is surrounded by National Forest, the town site itself is on private property. There is still small-scale mining going on today. To view the site, stay on the National Forest road. There are more buildings here than I anticipated. They are scattered over a large area, with many barely visible in the brush. Construction here spans a seventy-year period. While many are just flattened piles of lumber, enough are still standing to impress a visitor. These include the five-story hotel from 1924 and the 124-year-old mill. Remains of bridges from the wagon road and timbers from the old water flume mark the way to the site.

The country around Yellowjacket is breathtakingly beautiful. You should have a pickup truck, a full tank of fuel, and good weather to visit the site. The biggest challenge for me at the time was not to get cut off by the forest fires burning nearby. The fire was close enough to smell it; you could even taste the burning wood in the air.

SEVEN DEVILS MOUNTAINS

The Seven Devils Mountains, a string of semi-arid and forested mountains along the Snake River, have much to offer. Most of the land is National Forest, and this allows for a variety of outdoor activities to be available here.

Satan seems to be lurking all over the West. Everywhere you go, something is named devil this or hell that. It is a mystery how this place received such a name as Seven Devils. There are a lot of theories and legends, but no one really knows where the name comes from.

Mining of all types has been conducted in these mountains, but most historically significant was the turn-of-the-century copper rush. A fair number of mining towns sprang up in these mountains during the boom. The boom came to an end due to high development costs, transportation problems, and competition from Butte, Montana. Today, little or nothing remains of many of these boomtowns, but a few are still worth a visit.

Some precautions hiking there: first, take plenty of water because of high altitude combined with a semi-arid environment; second, keep an eye open for black bears, as they are numerous. Twice while in these mountains, I have had to deal with an overly curious male black bear in my camp.

There were several sites I did not visit. According to citizens in Cuprum, the town site of Helena burned down in a forest fire, leaving only the mine portal. Iron Springs, Paradise, and Rankins Mill are located together in the northern portion of these mountains, and all of them require a four-wheel drive vehicle or a hike to reach. By the early 1970s, little remained of these places, and it is likely they have disappeared with time. The country here and its high mountain lakes are some of the most beautiful of the Seven Devils Mountains.

Mineral City was in the southern end of the mountains. It requires an ATV or a long hike to reach, and again, little or nothing remains of the town. All these locations were boomtowns during the 1880–90s copper rush.

The town of Council provides the easiest approach to the ghost towns of the Seven Devils Mountains. Council also has gas stations, restaurants, stores, a museum, and a National Forest district office.

CUPRUM (Adams)
ALTITUDE 4,276 FEET

Cuprum, its name meaning copper in Latin, was the largest and longest-lasting boomtown of the Seven Devils Mountains copper rush. Today, it is mostly a sleepy collection of summer cottages.

Top: Wildlife is dangerous—do not approach!
Bottom: Mountain driving has its hazards.

Top: This building used to shake to the sound of dancing and music.

Bottom: A leftover from Cuprum's busier tourist days.

Right: The Copper Lodge, an establishment that Gary Cooper may have once visited.

In 1897 a hospital for miners and a post office were established. A regular mail route ran from Cuprum to Iron Springs, higher in the mountains. The place ballooned to five thousand people with a lodge, two large hotels, three brothels, a church, school, grocer, community hall, sawmill, post office, livery stable, restaurants, saloons, stores, and a stage.

The peak was in 1898, but things went bust in 1903 during the big crash. The rugged topography of the Seven Devils Mountains made transportation difficult, railroad construction impossible, and increased development costs. High mining and transportation costs kept the miners from being able to compete with Butte, Montana.

A small amount of mining, including gold, is still carried out in the area, but the major industries now are logging and tourism. The town has been damaged by major fires three times in its history; for this reason, there are no original buildings here. The oldest surviving building dates from 1909. Two of the more interesting and historic buildings are Skip's Dance Hall and the Copper Lodge.

Gary Cooper, who was a Montana cowboy before he was a Hollywood movie star, used to hunt black bear in the area. People in town still have his photo on their walls.

DECORAH (Adams)

Sitting on a road junction between Cuprum and Landore was the bawdy town of Decorah. The road spur that created the intersection here came from the mining town of Helena. Nearby, up Garnet Creek, were the Blue Jacket Mine and its mining camp. In between the mine and Decorah was the tiny three-cabin settlement of Garnet Town. Also, the road was a mail and stagecoach route. This made Decorah an excellent business location for its numerous saloons.

The town was officially established in 1901 when its post office opened, although it probably existed as a camp and way station as early as 1897. The town sat at the bottom of a wooded canyon next to Indian Creek. In the early days of the camp, the creek was placer mined. The peak population was probably 125. The post office closed at the end of 1902. Most of the businesses moved a mile up Indian Creek to Landore during 1903. A small number of saloons hung on here for a while, and Decorah eventually just faded away.

Today, all that remains are one historical sign facing the creek and, up the road, one log structure that may have been a saloon.

This large log building might have been one of the saloons of this bawdy town.

LANDORE (Adams)

Thomas G. Jones created Landore as a copper mining boomtown in 1898. He filed a claim near the busy Arkansas Mine, and instead of mining, laid out lots for a town. It worked. There were many other busy mines in the area along Indian Creek. The area and its newest town boomed.

Ore was hauled out in freight wagons, and on their return trips, they brought in equipment and supplies. There was a daily stage that left for the town of Council. A mail route ran through the settlement since 1897, but for a while, the nearest post office was in Cuprum. A weekly newspaper was printed, and on February 13, 1901, a post office was established. In 1903, the town of Decorah, a competitor for trade, faded out, and most of its businesses moved to Landore.

A smelter with a tall brick chimney was built in 1904 so that the ore could be processed here instead of being hauled out in freight wagons. It has been disassembled and hauled in from the silver mining town of Mineral City in Washington County. The smelter would operate sporadically for the next few years. Several attempts to run it on wood or to import coke as fuel were less than successful. By 1905, the town's population peaked between one thousand to three thousand. At about this time, a copper mine in Butte, Montana, put most other copper mines in the West out of business.

Landore died a slow death. Low copper prices caused the mines to close one by one. The smelter never showed a profit. The post office and Landore were both finished in 1916. In 1926, fraudulent promotion of properties raised hopes momentarily, only to see the bubble quickly burst.

This site is on private property surrounded by National Forest. One old cabin that is still in use is visible from the road. A National Forest historical marker that designates the sites was missing on my visit.

I could not see if remains of the smelter, such as its brick chimney, were still around. I believe there was a small amount of scattered, shattered remains on or around the property. Please do not trespass. Get permission to enter the site, or view it from the National Forest boundary line.

PLACER BASIN (Adams)

This was a place in the Seven Devils Mountains that, instead of joining the copper boom, mined gold. Arthur Frenchie David discovered the yellow metal here in 1882. He started the Placer Basin Gold Mine. It yielded a small quantity of high-grade ore, but work was sporadic and the total yield too small to continue.

All that remains of the mill and its buildings. The pines hide numerous foundations and concrete buttresses.

In 1905, a mill was built, but it ran only one summer. The crushed ore was hauled out by wagon to the railroad at Council.

The next boom came in the early 1930s when a prospector by the name of Tom Williams discovered another ore-bearing ledge. A few families and prospectors lived here in between these bursts of activity.

Claims were bought up, and the new owners developed the site. A second larger mill and a number of other buildings were constructed. The mill was in operation only during 1935 and 1936. Gold prices were up because of the Depression, and the mill produced millions of dollars worth of free milling gold. The mill did not open for the 1937 mining season, and eventually its machinery was salvaged and hauled away. The mill structure was standing into the late 1970s.

Placer Basin is misnamed. It was neither a true placer operation nor in a basin. Gold was obtained by crushing rock in the mill, and the town's location is on the side of a mountain. Life here was primitive for the families. Remains of their rugged lifestyle litter the old town site. The town had no post office, instead relying on exchanging mail with a postal rider. A mail route ran from Landore to Iron Springs. The road ran right through Placer Basin. Wagons hauled the mail during summer and fall, but when the snow began to fall, they used sleighs. When the mail wagon would approach, neighbors would call out announcing its arrival, then people would step out in the town's only street. They would signal by simply holding their outgoing mail high in the air or yelling out their own last name to the driver in the hopes that they might be receiving mail. Not high-tech, but it worked.

Winters here can be rough, and much of the town's population would leave for the season. Places like Council, which sits at a much lower altitude, would balloon from the flood of miners seeking a milder winter.

Household debris strewn among the boards reveals that this pile of lumber used to be a residence.

The remains of Placer Basin can be found on National Forest Road #112, four miles north of where it intersects National Forest Road #105. I used the intersection as a camping site. These roads were part of the old mail route.

The town site is marked by a historical sign, overgrown by trees and brush, and bisected by National Forest Road #105. Remains include the concrete foundation of the second mill, numerous collapsed buildings, and a lot of debris. Some of the buildings were homes; others were mining buildings. A lot of the construction was done with rough-hewn lumber. The debris comes from both household use and mining operations.

On the hike in, I saw old log cabins and water diversion canals along the route. I also saw a set of tracks in the dust from a very large bear. They proceeded in front of me and were fresh. These prints probably belonged to the same black bear that visited my camp later that evening.

SILVER AND LABOR STRIKES

Idaho's mineral wealth is spread throughout the whole state. In the northern part of the state, "Silver!" was frequently the call. During 1884, rich lead-silver lodes were discovered in Canyon Creek, just north of present-day Wallace, Idaho. Canyon Creek is steep, rugged, and beautiful. This is a very narrow canyon—only three hundred feet wide at its center. This had a dramatic effect on development. Towns quickly sprang up, growing dramatically in length up and down the canyon.

Two of them were Burke and Gem. The two flourished and died together. It may have had a silver lining, but a dark cloud hung over this valley. One problem this area had that was common in Northern Idaho at the time was labor strife. It would hit the mining industry hard here in the 1890s and the timber industry at the turn of the century.

Today, the area has other problems: the disappearance of cheap ore, frequent forest fires and flash floods, and tourists. The tourist problems include, but are not limited to, arson, graffiti, littering, souvenir hunting, theft, and vandalism.

The shallow ores have been played out, so the miners have to dig deeper. This is more expensive and more dangerous. This region has had more than its share of mine disasters. The fires and floods in the valley were easy to figure: towns full of steam engines belching sparks from smokestacks surrounded by mountains of pine forest that dry out every summer. Additionally, they were in a narrow mountain valley with streams running under, next to, around, and through Main Street. It was not a question of whether these towns would flood, but how frequently. A developed area prone to flash floods has the added deadly dimensions of no warning and hazardous debris churning in the water.

If you decide to visit the area for ghost town hunting or any other outdoor adventures, stop in at Wallace. It is on Interstate 90, so it is easy to find and access. The town has most of the services you might need and is located just south of Creek Canyon and its ghost towns. Wallace makes a nice stop in its own right. Downtown fills the valley floor with old multistory brick buildings, and the steep wooded mountainsides are crowded with perching houses.

The Wallace Visitor Center—a good place to start when you visit this beautiful town.

This is small-town America at its best. It looks like something Norman Rockwell would have painted. In fact, it was used as a movie set for the film *Dante's Peak*. There is a museum in town that has a good portion of its space dedicated to this cinematic event. Another museum in town, the Oasis, is dedicated to western gentlemen's clubs or brothels. There is even a hotel (the Jamieson Inn) that claims to be haunted.

Top: The massive Hecla Mine works.
Bottom: Many structures were built on the steep valley walls.

Besides camping, hunting, and trout fishing, the area is known for great mountain bike trails.

BURKE (Shoshone)

Lead-silver lode discoveries north of Wallace in 1884 led to rapid, heavy mining development. The silver mining town of Burke got started in 1885 and was named in honor of John M. Burke. A lot of money was poured into the mining operation here, and an influx of miners flooded the canyon. A railroad spur was completed to Burke in 1887. Soon, the new community was bursting at the seams.

During 1888, S. S. Glidden built the Tiger Hotel in the heart of town. The valley was narrow and its floor totally occupied by a road, railroad, and Canyon Creek. Their engineering solution was as wild as it was simple: they merely built over everything. All three actually ran through the center of the hotel. In the 1890s, a second railroad arrived and, having no other option, ran its tracks in the town's only street and right through the hotel lobby. This overcrowding caused fire hazards, traffic problems, ghastly accidents, and some interesting stories. One story has it that railroad brakemen would lift cooling pies from kitchen windowsills without even leaving the moving trains.

One big mine, the Tiger, employed only unmarried miners. These men were required to room and board in the company boardinghouse. Room and meals were automatically deducted from their pay. At its peak, the operation employed three hundred miners. The town of Burke seems to have been cursed to suffer. Even during its glory days, Burke endured harsh winters, high crime, bad air, overcrowding, street accidents, train derailments, violent labor strikes, and feuding mine owners. Then things went from bad to worse. In 1910, a giant snow slide buried part of Burke and killed nineteen people. Late that summer of the same year, the big fire struck, blackening more than five hundred thousand acres and killing seventy-two people. Then in 1923, Burke was virtually destroyed in a town fire.

There is a small population in Burke, and it has grown weary of vandals and souvenir hunters. I was fortunate enough to have been given a private tour by a kind local citizen. She had quickly spotted me poking around town and wanted to know what I was doing. I showed my I.D., told her I was doing book research, and immediately had a helpful friend.

A great deal remains of Burke. Construction appears to span a seventy-year period. The town is dominated by the massive Hecla Mine. There is always talk of the mine reopening, but the EPA is more concerned about cleaning the creek canyon of heavy metal contaminants. I was shown a very old jail that had the appearance of a medieval dungeon. It was accompanied by the obligatory ghost story. I was also shown two damaged wall murals. They had a western theme and were painted by an artist named Breckenridge. The story was he would do a painting to pay his room and board or other bills he owed. The building owner didn't know when the paintings had been done or what bills they paid.

Numerous other buildings and foundations of various ages and condition line the valley for miles. Please stay out of the buildings. Some are in poor condition and, therefore, dangerous; also, they are private property.

Burke is marked on the state highway map and is situated about six miles northeast of Wallace. The town is astride Highway 4, a two-lane blacktop road.

DELTA (Shoshone)

A junction on the road to busier places, this site is located on Beaver Creek about ten miles north of Wallace.

It is claimed that at its peak, the population here was one thousand. Today, there is little trace of such a large population. When mining declined in the valley and most neighboring towns started to fade, Delta lost its business base and faded with the rest of them. The few

Top: This was the last retail business open in Burke.
Middle: Numerous walls and foundations show where many more buildings once stood.
Bottom: The Burke City jail had none of the comforts of home.

Top: Delta, once a boomtown, then a cross-roads village, now a ghost.

Middle: Abandoned buildings are unsafe to enter.

Bottom: Countless dilapidated structures hug the hill sites at Gem.

buildings that are left in Delta are vacant and are from the latter half of the twentieth century. It is possible that Delta was hit by the devastating 1910 fire that ravaged this area.

The location was for sale on my last visit. The name may have come from its location at the juncture of Trail Creek with Beaver Creek.

Delta is about a dozen miles north of Wallace on County Road #456. Today the town is totally vacant and for sale.

GEM (Shoshone)

Gem, located three miles northwest of Wallace, was established in 1886 and grew to a peak population of twenty-five hundred. Gem was one in a string of mining towns lining Canyon Creek.

Like the other towns (Burke and Mace), it was constricted by the Canyon it was in, and it lay at the mercy of Canyon Creek, which flowed through it. These towns also shared the same limited road network, the same railroad spur, and the same tendency toward labor violence. Gem led the Canyon Creek Valley—and maybe even the entire state of Idaho—in that last category.

On July 11, 1892, during a gun battle between union miners and a mining company, the four-story Frisco Mill was completely demolished by several boxes of dynamite. This led to a military occupation by one thousand soldiers and four months of martial law in the mining district.

One winter during the 1890s, there was a strike that shut down the entire valley. Management responded by replacing the miners with non-union labor. The union men responded violently, driving many non-union men out of town, barefoot into a mid-winter's night. Other men weren't so lucky. Some who were caught were dragged into the hills, stripped naked, and left to freeze to death.

The second major industry in Gem was saloons. The primary mines here were the Bunker Hill, the Frisco, and the Gem.

Today a lot remains of Gem, but most of its construction postdates the first boom period and is in bad condition. The Hecla Mining Company assay office is here and appears ready to reopen.

Gem is three miles northeast of Wallace on Highway 4. The town is still marked on the state highway map.

MACE (Shoshone)

Bookended by its bigger neighbors of Gem and Burke, the town of Mace has faded and been forgotten by most. This place grew up in the late 1880s silver boom. It sits in Creek Canyon midway between the town sites of Gem and Burke. Remains include foundations, a railroad bed, mining debris, and tailings. There are occupied homes here, but it is all a mere fraction of what was here in its crowded glory days when the population topped out between five hundred and one thousand. Highway 4 bisects the site. The highway department has not forgotten this place. There is a state highway sign that says "Entering Mace."

Numerous campgrounds are scattered through the area. Caution: this is bear country!

WHITE KNOB MOUNTAINS

The White Knob Mountains parallel the Big Lost River Valley on its western flank. Major mineral discoveries were made here in 1879, and by 1884 numerous small mining settlements were popping up. Mining continued in the area until the 1980s. Today, ranching and tourism dominate the area's economy.

The valley floor, unless irrigated, is sage desert. Mountains flank the valley on the east and west. Semi-arid pine forests dot their sides at the upper altitudes.

A good place to stop while ghost town hunting in the area is Mackay. The town can provide you with a full range of services and has a little museum that is stacked full with information on the local area and its mining boom. For those more adventurous, there is the Mine Hill Auto Loop Tour, a circular route on White Knob Mountain

The Mine Hill Loop Tour is more a maze than a loop, with some rough roads at that.

that takes you by numerous mining sites. These include the ghost towns of Cliff City and White Knob. Portions of this road are four-wheel drive only. I had to hike.

The only site I didn't visit here was that of Era, a silver-mining town that started in 1885. Its location is to the southeast of Mackay on Champagne Creek and is off the beaten track. All that is claimed to be left is the outline of the rock foundation of a rock-crushing mill.

CLIFF CITY (Custer)

Founded in a canyon along Cliff Creek in summer 1884, Cliff City was one of the first towns of the White Knob Mountain's copper boom. The name of the creek and town derives from the high cliffs that loom over them.

The Big Copper Mine, mill, and a fifty-ton, two-stack smelter were finished later that year, and the combination gave birth to a small local mining boom. The smelter was the first in the area. The mine was above the town on the south side of White Knob Mountain. There were numerous equipment and smelting problems here. The smelter was fueled with charcoal. The charcoal was made in pits in the creek bed just above town. Slaked lime was used to process the copper ore, and it was produced in kilns below town. Three of these kilns are still there today. When the smelter was running, this must have been a busy, noisy, smoky, smelly place. The smelter ran in three short spurts: first, from November 23, 1884, to early December 1884; second, from July 22, 1885, to January 1886; and third, from August 1890 to February 1891. Finally, Wayne Darlington took over the operations during the 1890s, and the smelter produced consistently into 1901. A larger smelter was built at this time in nearby Mackay. When this happened, there was no further use for the Cliff City smelter. The town started a slow fadeout.

It is claimed that the town had a peak population of about three hundred. If this is true, most lived in tents or dugouts. The town had only twenty houses by fall 1884. There were additional cabins next to the mines on the mountain above town. Cliff City also had a store, a small sawmill, and three saloons. Copper production and business in general were up and down like a roller coaster. By 1915, only a few families remained, and they were gone by the mid-1920s.

Remnants of the site are the foundation of the large mill, parts of the smelter, three kilns, and fragments of some cabins.

Cliff City's location, at the bottom of a canyon, is on the Mine Hill Tour Loop. To see the remains of this site, you either take a jeep or have to hike a rough trail a little more than a mile through high-altitude desert. Take water, and watch out for rattlesnakes. Much of this loop and these sites are on private property; please be respectful.

DARLINGTON (Butte)

Darlington was founded in 1901 by Wayne Darlington as a railroad town. He named the town after himself, of course, just like the Darlington Mine he had managed at White Knob.

The railroad went out of business in 1940. A highway replaced it and became the main source of commerce for the town. Some of the buildings here had been moved from the town of White Knob. During my visit in 2006, two businesses were still in operation. By 2007, they had closed, putting Darlington into the ranks of Idaho ghost towns. You might get a chuckle out of the miniature golf course with sagebrush between the holes. There are a couple of occupied homes in town. Respect the owners' property, please.

Darling is located twelve miles south of Mackay on Highway 93. The town is still marked on the official state highway map, making it easy to find.

MAMMOTH (Custer)

In Mammoth Canyon along Mammoth Creek are the bare remains of the small copper mining town of Mammoth. The ore from here was probably hauled out in freight wagons and smelted in Houston or Mackay. There was at least a small mill and some cabins here. I have found little history on this site. The trail in is rough and

Top: The Darlington Store, like most of the town, is for sale.

Middle: A miniature golf course set amid the sagebrush.

Bottom: This old gas station was converted to a house and is now vacant.

must be hiked. Take a camera, plenty of water, and watch out for rattlesnakes. The setting is isolated, rugged, and quite scenic. Remains are said to be ruins of cabins and a foundation from the mill. Old mines dot the mountainsides above Mammoth. This was a small development and its years of operation unknown to me, but construction here clearly shows it to be of an early period.

WHITE KNOB (Custer)

Historical sources disagree on a number of details but agree that White Knob started as a copper mine and town founded by Wayne Darlington. One book says summer 1899; another says 1900. A state tourist brochure says the town was incorporated in 1901. A historical marker at the site says it was founded in 1902.

The first manager of the White Knob Mine and company town was Wayne Darlington. Darlington and his workers did not get along—at all. After much arguing with Darlington, the workers decided to form a union and did so on April 4, 1902. This led to immediate confrontation. Darlington threatened to lock out or replace the union miners. Two days later, the miners went on strike and threw out Darlington, along with his manager and superintendent. The manager and superintendent left the area. Wayne Darlington went into the valley and founded a small railroad community, Darlington, Idaho.

The birth of the town of Mackay, with its smelters and railroad spur, made large-scale mining at White Knob feasible. Still, there were numerous problems—with the smelters, their furnaces, their fuel, the ore consistency, lumber shortages, and more. At first, ore was moved down the mountain to the smelters by wagon or pack mule. However, this was not a cost-effective manner of getting the ore to the smelters, and they were replaced by an electric small-gauge railroad. This helped a lot but did not solve the problem entirely.

The town grew to a population of a few hundred with stores, a post office, a boardinghouse, a pool hall, a barbershop, a restaurant, an

Top: This was the headhouse for the tramway.
Bottom: Only a handful of buildings still stand here.

amusement hall, a school, a theater, and many cabins, shacks, and outbuildings. The town went up and down with the mine, and the mine went up and down with copper prices. In 1905, it almost failed. Some years, the mine even closed due to low copper prices. What saved mining here was good management and reducing production costs.

The new management came from Frank M. Leland of California. He greatly reduced operating costs and introduced other business efficiencies. In 1905, he replaced the electric railway with a Shay steam locomotive, and this reduced the local railway cost to just one-fourth of its previous level. Then in 1906 he reworked the company's system with its lessors mining on the mountain. More importantly, with the help of a better assayer he hired, the smelting problems were solved. Instead of closing the mines they had been made profitable, and in only a two-year period. Finally, building the Taylor Sawmill solved the lumber problem and allowed for a steady supply of building materials and mine timbers. The mine and the town both grew steadily.

Most of what remains of the actual town of White Knob looks like this.

By 1915, White Knob had grown to a population of five hundred. By 1918, it had grown to one thousand, and the number of businesses had grown with it. These included a restaurant and a movie house. There was telephone and daily stagecoach service from Mackay. That year, a gravity-powered aerial tramway was completed. It greatly improved the delivery of ore from the mines to the smelters and completely replaced the Shay steam engines. The tramway operated until 1940. Parts of it still stand today and can be seen on the Mine Hill Tour.

The White Knob Mine closed in 1931, and most of the town emptied in 1932. The White Knob School lasted until 1940, serving the families still on Mine Hill. Most of the families left on Mine Hill were already sending their children to school in Mackay. Limited mining activity continued sporadically on the mountain until at least 1975. Almost a million tons of ore have been taken out of the mountain.

The White Knob town site is west of Mackay on White Knob Mountain. The site can be reached in your family car, weather permitting, and directions are available almost anywhere in Mackay. A lot remains of the mining operation, but the actual town is in bad shape. There are a few structures partially standing, but most are piles of sticks on the ground. These remains cover a fair area. The local historical society has a sign there. Careful: some of these buildings had basements.

YANKEE FORK MINING DISTRICT

The first group of prospectors came to this area in the early 1860s. They didn't find any gold, but they did get to name numerous features here. These prospectors were Yankee northerners and gave things northern names. One was a creek named the Yankee Fork. The mining district would take its name from this creek after gold was discovered in it during 1870. With the discovery, a horde of prospectors and merchants rushed to the area, and the boom was on. Eventually, placer mining gave way to hydraulic, dredge, and hard-rock mining. These new methods and market price fluctuations would lead to other "booms."

One legend of lost treasure in the Yankee Fork is the story of the "Lost Swim Lode." Isaac T. Swim, a son of a well-known Idaho family, claimed that on September 9, 1881, he had located a major gold deposit approximately fifteen miles south of Bonanza City. Winter weather was approaching, so Isaac gathered some choice gold nuggets as proof of his story and headed back to Bonanza. The next spring, when weather permitted, Isaac set out to relocate his claim. He was never heard from again. Some stories say he drowned

The winter weather and the state force most roads in this area to close for months.

crossing the Salmon. Another is that robbers ambushed him, but no one really knows.

The land here is scenic and rugged. There is a "bush pilot" doctor in the area that actually makes house calls by airplane. This is a place the Indians called "The Land of Deep Snows." Winter can bury the roads, along with everything else, under tons of snow, and even in August the nights are cool. Mining is still carried out here, although logging and tourism are also important to the local economy. There are numerous campgrounds and tens of thousands of acres of forest for primitive camping in the area.

Any visit to the area calls for a stop at the Yankee Fork Visitor Center outside Challis. The visitor center is informative and fun. It has a museum, a small movie theater, restrooms and more. You can even pan for gold there.

The Wells Fargo building.

BAYHORSE (Custer)

Bayhorse started in 1864 as a small gold placer camp. In the early 1870s, placer silver, followed by a few veins, was discovered here. Beginning in 1877, hard-rock mining for silver and lead was carried out. By 1878 it was being done on a large scale. Numerous mining tunnels were spread out amongst various mountain valleys. Soon timber mills, ore mills, a stamp mill and a smelter were built. The stamp mill and smelter were completed in 1880. Miners' cabins dotted the hillsides and Bayhorse was at the center of this beehive of activity. There was a main street lined with a large number of business buildings, constructed mostly with lumber. These included saloons, stores, boardinghouses, assay offices, banks and more. One building, the Wells Fargo, was built of stone. For added protection it had steel bars on the windows. It still stands today. So does the famous Bayhorse Saloon. Six beehive kilns were built during the boom years to make charcoal for the smelters. They are still here today.

A powder magazine for storing explosives used in the mine.

The town also had a post office, but initially the federal government rejected the town's application under the name Bayhorse. From 1883

Beehive kilns for making charcoal.

The old mill still stands at Bayhorse.

until at least 1885, the town was known as Aetna. Sometime before 1888, the postal service agreed to change the town's name back to Bayhorse. Many structures were lost on May 14, 1884, due to a large fire in the town's business section.

The peak years at Bayhorse were the 1880s and 1890s. After that, the mines became less productive, and all operations ceased by 1915. When the last mine shut down, the town was abandoned. The main mine and town reopened from 1920 through 1925. The mine opened again for short periods in 1935, 1967, and 1968.

While surrounded by National Forest, this has been private property. Please respect it. Until recently, there had been a caretaker here. I viewed most of the site from the National Forest road on my first two visits. The place had a "For Sale" sign up. Now it is the future site of a state historical park. On my second visit here, I suffered the indignity of getting stuck on a flat and level road. Simple reason: mud.

Behind Bayhorse and upcreek from the mill are mine roads, shafts, cabins, and all sorts of debris scattered over a large area. Just up

the road are the six beehive kilns. There are also two cemeteries here. One is along the road on the way to the kilns. The graves were fenced in to protect the interred bodies from being dug up by coyotes or wolves. The other cemetery is located somewhere below town. There are more than twenty structures left in the town and around the mill. These include the Bayhorse Saloon and the stone Wells Fargo building. Now that the state has possession of this ghost town, the land's future is ensured and, in the near future, will be a gem of a state historical site.

Bayhorse is southwest of Challis in the Salmon—Challis National Forest. It is marked on the National Forest maps and numerous other publications. More information may be obtained at the Yankee Fork Visitor Center. The site, when the road is dry, is accessible in your family car.

BONANZA (Custer)

The Yankee Fork's first permanent settlement was called Bonanza (Spanish for prosperity). Officially called Bonanza City, it started in 1876 as a camp by placer miners working the Yankee Fork and Jordan Creek. In early 1877, Charles Franklin officially established a town here. Starting in the fall, mule packers began trekking the eighty-four rough miles from Ketchum with machinery and supplies. A post office was established here on June 16, 1879, with William A. Morton as its first postmaster. It was the first post office in the district.

Top: Bonanza townsite.

Middle: An early mobile home.

Bottom: The peak looming in the background is Mount Greylock.

By 1881, the town had a post office, a mine, a dentist, a baseball diamond, a croquet field, a newspaper, the *Yankee Herald*, a tin shop, a watchmaker, a butcher shop, two general stores, a furniture shop, a hardware store, a café and dance hall (the Charles Franklin House), a two-story hotel (the Dodge), and at least nine saloons, one hundred homes and between six hundred to fifteen hundred residents. The main business streets were lined with boardwalks or wooden sidewalks so the customers would not have to walk in the mud or snow. Bonanza had become the business and social center for the Yankee Fork Mining District. At first, the town was kept supplied by trains of pack mules operating from Challis and Ketchum. By 1880, a toll road from Challis reached the community.

Even though the city had a public well and water system, large fires in 1889 and 1897 destroyed most of Bonanza. After the fires a number of people and most of the surviving businesses moved to neighboring Custer. When the last local mine closed in 1911, Bonanza became a ghost. The 1930s saw a small rebirth of sorts. With higher Depression-era gold prices, miners drifted back to the area to rework a number of claims. With them they brought what can only be described as "mobile homes." Some of them are still there today. They have been put together from all sorts of materials and items. The sides and roofs are of corrugated metal, and the wheels belonged to ore carts or railroad cars. Some homes also had screen doors and windows. It seems some miners were finally noticing their lifestyle in the mining industry was transient in nature.

In 1934 the Civilian Conservation Corps built the Bonanza CCC Camp on part of the old town site and, among other endeavors, built the National Forest Guard Station here. Last, from 1939 to 1952 a handful of men lived in the area to operate the Yankee Fork Dredge. The dredge operation ran from October 1939 to November 1942 and again from late 1945 to 1953.

While doing research and camping in this area I have spent the night in Bonanza and both its cemeteries. One of the two cemeteries was a "boot hill" and has a very interesting history. Originally, the site was chosen as Bonanza's new cemetery, but after the first three bodies were buried in it, no one wanted anything to do with it, so, the cemetery became a boot hill with a story to be told around the campfire or on Halloween night.

Gold rushes can attract people from all over the world, and this one lured Richard King and Agnes Elizabeth King from London, England. They were a married couple and chose to set up a saloon in Bonanza City. Richard played the real estate market here. Elizabeth was a social butterfly who everyone called "Liz." The couple eventually became

One of many times I've spent the night in the ghost town's cemetery.

friends with the hotel owner and town founder, Charles Franklin. It has been rumored that Liz and Charles were having an affair.

Richard was shot and killed on July 14, 1879. A business partner killed him during an argument. Charles Franklin and Elizabeth King purchased two graves in the new town cemetery, and Richard was buried in one of them.

Very soon after Richard's burial, Charles and Elizabeth began to openly date one another. Then a poker dealer by the name of Robert Hawthorne drifted into town. In a short time, Liz dropped Charles and started dating the poker dealer. After a short courtship, the two were married. The town was shocked and abuzz with talk. More was to come. On August 11, 1880, six days after the pair were married, they were found shot to death. It was murder. The number one suspect for the double murder was Charles Franklin, but nothing could be proven. Franklin arranged to have the pair buried in the new cemetery with Richard King. He had Elizabeth buried between her two husbands. He also had the last name of King used instead of Hawthorne on Liz's grave marker, and instead of her date of death being recorded, the date of her marriage to Hawthorne was placed on the headstone.

Main cemetery of Bonanza.

A short while thereafter, Charles Franklin left his business and the town he helped found and was never heard of again. Legend claims that the sobbing figure of a woman has been seen placing flowers on one or both of the graves of the two husbands. The legend says the visiting female phantom is the broken-hearted spirit of Elizabeth Hawthorne. If Liz visited during my camp stay here, she failed to wake me.

Bonanza is north of Sunbeam on Yankee Fork Road. In addition to the trailers mentioned before, there are about a dozen other buildings or their collapsed skeletons that have survived fire, time, and tourist. Some of these are early-period log cabin construction. Historical markers are spread out over the site. Some of the sites are on private property and marked; please treat them as such. The two cemeteries

A portion of the old Custer townsite is now an outdoor museum.

are west of town on National Forest Road #74. The town site and cemeteries are all marked on the Challis National Forest map.

CUSTER (Custer County)

A true gem, this ghost town is an outdoor museum operated by the National Forest Service.

Gold ores were found in the mountains around the Yankee Fork and Jordan Creek in 1875, and claims were quickly staked out. The richest claim was discovered by three prospectors on August 17, 1876, and called the General Custer.

Custer started as a gold mining camp in 1876. It is situated on the north side of Mackay Creek about two miles above Bonanza. In 1879, lots were laid out by Samuel "Sammy" Halman, and a new town was officially established. It was named Custer after the largest mine of the area, the General Custer. The town grew steadily with the development of numerous quartz mines in the hills above. The first boom lasted until the late 1880s. Deforestation and operating costs of deep mines were hindering mining. The deforestation led to numerous snow slides and even a few deaths at Custer.

At first, the site was serviced solely by mule trains. By 1880, a toll road over Mill Creek from Challis was finished. It allowed freight wagons to haul in heavier loads. The Custer Mill opened up in 1881. A newspaper (the *Prospector*) was published here during the early 1880s. A tramway was built up the hillside to bring ore down from the mines that overlooked Custer. At its peak, the mill had thirty stamps working. The first boom peaked here in 1888. At that time, the population was claimed to be as high as thirty-nine hundred. The business community servicing the miners was large. It boasted a bakery, three general stores, two restaurants, two liveries, a butcher shop, three rooming houses, two barbershops, a furniture store, a carpenter shop, a blacksmith, a Wells Fargo office, two Chinese laundries, a Chinese goods store, a hotel (the Nevada House), and for entertainment, a dance hall, four red-light houses, and five saloons.

Some of what remains of
Custer is on private property.

In 1895, Custer experienced a second short boom. A miner's strike in
1897 slowed things considerably. Also, in 1897, fire had destroyed a
large part of neighboring Bonanza and many of its businesses left for
Custer, making it the commercial and cultural center for the area.

By 1900 a third wave of prosperity was cresting. Custer had a school,
jail, miners' union hall, post office, assay office, blacksmith shop,
icehouse, stores, saloons, and bawdy houses. It also had a ski slope
and playing fields for baseball and croquet. The town even had
its own baseball team. By this time the town was becoming more
family-oriented. There was still a small Chinatown at the south end
of Main Street. The mill closed down in 1903; it has since burned
down but its foundation and parts of the tramway are still visible.
After that the community faded. In fall 1910, the post office closed
and the town became a ghost.

At one time, Bonanza and Custer grew so large, they almost met.
At times the communities even shared parts of their government.
The Mike Spawn Brewery was built between the two and it supplied
beer to saloons in both towns. Bonanza even shared its cemetery
with some of the deceased from Custer. Some published sources
state Custer did not have a cemetery. This is not true; in fact, it had
three. One of these contains the bodies of the first two babies born

Workings of a five-stamp rock crusher.

First: McFadden. The building at the top of the photo has been propped up and a roof emplaced for its preservation.

Second: Remains of a corduroy road.

Third: Too large for a miner's cabin—this building had multiple stories and numerous windows.

Fourth: Square nails and lead cans date this site to 1884 or earlier.

in Custer. Still, some of Custer's residents were buried in the main Bonanza cemetery.

The U.S. Forest Service operates a museum in the old one-room schoolhouse here and a gift shop is across the street in an old saloon. "Custer Days" is celebrated on the second Saturday in July.

MCFADDEN (Custer)

This ghost town is little known, very remote, and hard to find. Yet, on my trip, there was much evidence of abuse to the site. On this visit I spotted three rock rings used for campfires that contained boards or logs from the town's more than 120-year-old buildings.

The site, like many Idaho mining camps, is a narrow mountain valley with a mountain stream running down the center. I could not find a map that showed the location nor very much history about the town.

McFadden popped up in 1880 as a gold and silver mining camp. Following placer deposits up Eightmile Creek, a lode deposit was located on the west bank and it became the McFadden Mine. Colonel James McFadden owned the mine. Lead was also recovered during the silver mining.

The town had a post office from 1900 through 1901. Its one and only postmaster was a woman with the last name of McFadden. It was a one-street town with a small number of businesses and cabins on both sides. There was a small water-powered mill just downstream of town, and a few bare beams and boards remain as evidence.

The road to McFadden feeds into the Custer Motorway and is interesting in itself. In several places Eightmile Creek or mountain springs turn the road into a bog. To overcome these obstacles the pioneers used an old-time solution—corduroy roads. These are roads built of layers of logs laid parallel to one another. You can still see rotting logs on sections of the road. There were at least three bridges on this byway, but only decaying fragments remain. These obstacles make it best to hike in. At one river crossing is a log structure. It is much larger than your average miner's cabin and was constructed with no nails. The roof has caved in but the walls were still standing. The mud in the road allowed for a fine study in animal tracks, which on the day I hiked in included those of a wolf.

Remains here are eight standing structures and a handful of collapsed structures. Both round and square nails were used in construction. Examination of debris included lead cans dating back to at least 1880.

SUNBEAM (Custer)

Sunbeam was a town, dam, steam house, old mine and mining camp. Today the name is used by both a modern mining operation and a country store. A community called Sunbeam is shown on the Idaho state highway map. This is the location of the Sunbeam store and the Sunbeam Dam. The store also has a restaurant and cabins. It started as a pioneer cabin site, became a store, and then grew into a small town. This place was first named Junction Bar. Today nothing remains of the old town. The Sunbeam store is a good stop for most services.

Ebenezer Cunningham built the cabin in 1881. The Sunbeam Mine, discovered in 1876, was the first to use the name; everything else was named after the mine. The dam was completed in 1910. The dam had a hydroelectrical generating power plant. It was built to provide power for the Sunbeam Mill. Electric power was not common in those days and even more uncommon in a place like rural Idaho. Wood and water mills had been used as virtually the only sources of energy and deforestation was causing a shortage of wood.

How ironic: just as the lights were going out in both Bonanza and Custer, electricity was brought to the area. This boom went bust fast. The Sunbeam Mill opened in 1911 and closed after operating only one month. The Sunbeam Mine Company was forced into bankruptcy and its equipment was removed. Later on, the dam

was breached with dynamite to allow the continued migration of salmon upstream. Today there is nothing left of the mill but the dam remains for viewing. It is across the highway from the Sunbeam store. There is a parking lot, historical markers, and an overlook of the dam.

During the 1930s a CCC company built the Sunbeam Bathhouse. It is just upstream from the dam and up the highway. The structure still stands and is preserved as a historical site. The bathhouse was built with local stone and water piped in from a naturally hot spring. The spring is separated from the bathhouse by the highway. If you visit here, watch for traffic. If you drive through, watch out for pedestrians. Caution: in cold weather, mist from the hot spring can form ice on the road.

Today a modern and massive open-air mining operation located up Jordan Creek is also called Sunbeam. Just across the valley from the modern mine is an old mining camp. It is not confirmed, but it too may also have been named Sunbeam. I found it while hiking one day. Besides the mine tunnel, there were twelve cabins and a company combination office and store. Construction appeared to date from the 1920s.

YANKEE FORK DREDGE (Custer)

During 1939 the Yankee Fork Creek was tested for the viability of dredge-mining the stream. The Snake River Mining Company did the tests. The results were good enough that the Bucyrus-Erie Company was contracted to build a dredge. The disassembled dredge parts were first shipped by rail to Mackay. From there, they were hauled by trucks to the Yankee Fork and then assembled during 1940.

The dredge's dimensions are impressive; it is 112 feet long, 64 feet high, 54 feet wide and weighs 988 tons. Its 71 buckets can each hold 8 cubic yards of earth. The dredge assembly and startup preparation took from April 1, 1939, to August 24, 1940. After that the dredge started to work its way up Jordan Creek. During early 1942 all

The teeth of the operation.
Photo by Karen Bloodworth.

operations were forced to cease by the federal government due to its being nonessential to the war effort. With the end of WWII, operations were restarted late in 1945. During 1947 the Snake River Mining Company offered the dredge for sale, and in 1949 J. R. Simplot bought the entire operation for just $75,000.

He operated the dredge until fall 1952, then shut it down. In 1953 it was discovered to be accidentally on the wrong property, so it was restarted and moved back onto the correct claim and shut down for the last time.

Evidence of the dredging operation is plainly visible in the form of dredge tailings extending five and a half miles from Pole Flat Campground to the mouth of Jordan Creek. The tailings were left behind as the dredge moved upstream.

The dredge still rests today where it was finally shut down in 1953. It has been partially restored and operates as a museum during the summer seasons. The dredge is located midway between the ghost towns of Bonanza and Custer.

Yankee Fork Dredge.

ALL THE REST

Wildlife can be a road hazard. I spotted these sheep near Shoup. The male at left noticed me before I spotted him.

My first three attempts to reach Atlanta were thwarted when the road was closed due to flood, landslide, or forest fire. The road is frequently closed by snow for months at a time.

ATLANTA (Elmore)

Atlanta is one of Idaho's oldest towns. Placer gold was discovered in a creek here in early August 1863. The men tried to keep their discovery a secret, but it didn't last long. The group returned quietly the next season but their preparations had created some curiosity. When they organized their claims into the Yuba River mining district, it instantly attracted more than one hundred other gold prospectors. A lode discovery was made and a town established in late 1864.

Confederate sympathizers for the Battle of Atlanta named the town. They mistakenly believed that the battle had been a southern victory when, in actuality, it was General Sherman and the North that had won the battle. Whatever the history, the name stuck.

For the first few years mining was limited because the town had only arrastras and a few small-scale stamp mills to crush or process the ore. The first large-scale stamp mill started operations during summer 1867. First, the mill broke down, then it was discovered that the amalgamator did not function properly. For the next decade there were numerous failures and setbacks. Finally, in 1877, one mill was operating successfully. In 1878 a road was completed from Rocky Bar and this spurred further development. From 1908 to 1910 a cyanide separation plant operated here successfully. Mining operations were greatly improved in 1932 when a modern amalgamation-flotation concentrator was installed. From 1932 to 1936, the Atlanta Mining District was the leading Idaho gold producer until WWII stopped gold production. The Talache Mine operated in Atlanta from 1947 to 1953. It produced both gold and antimony.

Today there are many original structures here. Some are dilapidated, others converted from the original use. At the same time brand new construction is mixed in parts of town. A number of the older buildings have been moved in from another nearby ghost town, Rocky Bar.

One cluster of buildings belongs to the National Forest Service. One cabin there is a rental belonging to the National Reservation System. I spent three hot days there one August and had the pleasure of talking with Charlie Swearingen. He was working there for the National Forest Service and provided me with much information about Atlanta and the Boise Basin. There is a small year-round population in Atlanta that balloons in the summer.

This is an isolated spot at the end of the road; what's more, most of the people here like it that way. The community is served by a small airstrip and heliport. In town, there is an inn with rooms, a bar, and a restaurant. My request for a menu produced a series of chuckles from the locals. It is not so much a question of what they can cook but more of what they have on stock in the kitchen.

You can approach Atlanta from three different routes; the best is from Highway 21 just south of the Lowman Pass. Snow and roads washed out or closed due to a landslide turned me back on my first three attempts to reach Atlanta. All along the route you will see vast devastation from recent forest fires. Atlanta is shown on the state highway map.

Top: Numerous old cabins are used as summer cottages.

Middle: This was the only retail business left open in town. A couple of others had recently closed. P.S.: The dogs formed a welcoming committee.

Bottom: This is one of a number of structures moved here from Rocky Bar.

BANNER CITY (Boise)

In 1864, while looking for a better route to Rocky Bar, James Hawley and Jess Bradford discovered a rich silver lode. They named it the Banner Lode and quickly sold their claim. The new owner was an Idaho City merchant who controlled the Elmira Silver Company. His name was Crafts. At first the site was called Silver City, then Banner. Two other towns, Eureka and Forest City, popped up in the area due to this mineral discovery. During Banner's first winter, 1864–65, the town was cut off from the outside world by eight feet of snow. Lack of roads and railways held back development for a number of years. Through the Elmira Silver Company a great deal of money, much of it English, was spent designing and building the site.

In 1872 a twenty-stamp Fraser and Chalmers mill was freighted in from Kansas City. A cable tramway was built to bring down ore from the mountain. It ran from the mile-long Banner Mine to the new stamp mill. This expansion saw the town's name expanded to Banner City. The city came with a new post office, livery, at least one saloon, and possibly a stage station. Still, development was slow and major production of ore was not achieved until after 1882. The mine was the basis of the town's economy and when it closed, so did the town.

The Banner was the only really productive silver mine in the area. The Elmira Silver Mining Company ran a successful operation here for a number of years. Eventually the mine ran too deep and became too expensive to operate. It shut down in 1921 and the post office closed with it. Then the route was changed for the road out of Idaho City. The town died. One cabin remained occupied by a prospector for a good number of years.

Today, what little that remains is blending back into the earth. A row of what used to be miners' cabins is visible as irregular piles of old timber with trees and willow bushes growing up out of them. One was supposed to have been a saloon.

Other remains are two collapsed buildings. One is said to have been the livery barn, the other the post office. A short distance away is a row of woodpiles with clumps of trees growing in them, it's all that remains of a row of cabins.

Banner is located in the Boise National Forest, southeast of Lowman. The site is marked on the Boise National Forest Map, Delorme State Highway Atlas, and the topo map of the area. To find it you must be able to read these maps and navigate the maze of National Forest mountain roads, which are gravel and well maintained. The environment is semi-dry, mountainous pine forests with elevations ranging from 7,700 to 8,200 feet. The Lowman fire during 2007 threatened the whole area.

BOULDER CITY (Blaine)

In 1878 lead/silver deposits were discovered in the Boulder Basin area. This led to further explorations.

During 1879 prospectors found gold in what would be called Boulder Creek and quickly traced its source to the stream's headwaters, Boulder Peak. This mountain looms over the abandoned town site and is dotted with old mining tunnels. At least one mine, the Sorensen, had a gravity-fed tramway to bring ore down from the mountain to a rock crusher. Heavy four-foot-high metal buckets were used. Miners would use the tram to commute up the mountain to

Left: Remains of the Golden Glow Mill.

Top: Remains of the tramway operations.

Middle: This was a two-story hotel. This is the spot where I enjoyed my backpack lunch of dehydrated fruit and twenty-year-old Army combat rations, aka MREs.

Bottom: Most of the logs on this cabin were cut with an ax instead of being sawed.

work. The weight of a loaded ore bucket coming downhill powered the ride, and what a ride it must have been. When the ore reached the bottom it was dumped, the rock crushed and then turned onto shaker tables. The tables were built over Boulder Creek. This way the crushed rock was washed and the slag sluiced off. It could be done only during the summer since the stream froze over every winter. Snow could linger to the next winter. Other major mines here were the Bazouk, Boulder, Golden Glow, Ophir, Sullivan, and Tip Top.

The area, known as Boulder Basin, is isolated, rocky and windswept. It was not a place to settle if not for the gold. At first supplies were packed in by mule, but with time a rough road allowed for freight to be hauled in and ore out by wagon. A small town quickly popped up below the mountain peak and its numerous mines. It was the second town established in the Wood River Valley. The wagon road is now the main hiking trail into the Basin.

A look back on the hike to Boulder City.

Later, the town was renamed Briggs. This was done for "postal" reasons. Booming from 1880 to 1888, the town had a hotel, post office, corral, saloon, store and an ore-processing mill. Remains are the Boulder Basin Mill, the Golden Glow mining camp, ruins of a tram, mechanical sluice boxes, miners' cabins and a two-story log cabin that probably was the hotel at Briggs. Other mines and equipment dot the basin. Both the old pack trail and wagon road lead into the site.

The way I took to this site is over a seven-mile jeep road and hiking trail. At one time it was the wagon road in. Along the way I saw mine tailings, the ruins of a small mill next to Boulder Creek and two-story log structures, one of which appears to have been a barn and stable. It is a very beautiful alpine setting with spring flowers blooming in August. I had a dehydrated picnic lunch here myself. Elevation is 9,300 feet, depending on where you're standing in town.

The turnoff to Boulder City is on the east side of Highway 75, about twelve miles north of Ketchum. The turn is supposed to be marked but it wasn't on my visit. You turn onto National Forest Road #184. After about two miles you intersect with and turn right onto National Forest Road #158. You take it for five more miles, all uphill to Boulder City. These really aren't roads but boulder-strewn hiking trails. This place gets more visitors than you might think. On my visit I encountered three campers, two hikers and two ATV-ers. I had nice conversations with all of them. The National Forest trail sign-in book showed numerous visitors to the Basin during the summer.

There are several beautiful alpine lakes in this mountain basin but because the lakes freeze solid most winters they have no fish in them. At the head of one of these lakes are steep cliffs that the swallows of San Juan Capistrano return to each spring and nest on. A twelve-foot-high cross constructed of heavy timber had been built on top of the cliffs overlooking the unnamed lake. It is unknown who constructed the cross or when it was erected. It is also unknown who the vandals were who cut it down and burned it for firewood.

Interesting travel note: while setting up my base camp I was joined by a rather large fox. It simply walked into my camp and sat down less than ten feet from me. It eventually left, only to rejoin me later that evening on a walk. It walked alongside me as if it were a pet. Later on it returned to my base camp yet again and lay next to the picnic bench while I set up my sleeping cot. The conversation wasn't much but the company was still pleasant.

BOULDER CITY (Boundary)

This is a town site with an interesting though sketchy history. It started as a gold mining camp in 1884. Placer deposits had been discovered here in Boulder Creek, hence the town's name. By the early 1900s the placer deposits had played out and people had moved on. Between 1908 and 1910 the Idaho Gold and Radium Company developed a mine and built a company town at the site. There was a bank, a school, a company store, and according to one source, a post office. The company also built a sawmill to provide lumber for houses and the other buildings.

The owner of the mining company and founder and promoter of the town was Mr. J. M. Schnatterly. He claimed to have discovered a fifteen-inch-wide vein of radium here. If true, this would have been the richest vein of radium in the world at that time. To promote his company Mr. Schnatterly would bring potential investors to the mine site. First, they would take a train to Bonners Ferry. From there Mr. Schnatterly would literally take his prospective investors for a boat ride. It was up the Kootenai River in his private launch to Leonia and from there, a buggy ride to the mine. It seems that no one except Schnatterly claims to have ever seen the vein. After raising $2 million in capital through his promotions, no mention of radium was ever heard again.

The town also had a small cemetery. Its location is about a mile down the road from the town site. At one time the mine's name here was the Idamont mine. Nothing like radium was ever mined here, and more was spent developing the site than was taken out any gold. The town soon faded for a second time.

The next story I have only one source for. It was a telephone interview with a National Forest employee and I have yet to confirm the claims. It begins in the early 1920s; it was claimed there were rubies and an investment group was formed. Scam, hoax or mistake, there were no rubies. Before things were completely sorted out, the founder of the venture was blown up in his boat. It is unclear if the explosion was accidental or due to suicide or even murder. Local legend says the body was never recovered. After that, the town was truly finished.

In the late 1990s two buildings were still standing but they might be gone now. One was the school. Some foundations are still here, including the banks. The remains of the cemetery and mine are also nearby. The National Forest Service has replaced the original stone grave markers with wooden ones. This was due to vandalism at the cemetery and the rest of the site. A road runs alongside the old town site. This makes both access and vandalism easy.

One important side note: grizzly bears are active in this area.

What's left of the town is a short walk off the road into the woods. The roads into the area are mostly four-wheel drive and require good navigational skills. The location is marked on the Panhandle National Forest map. If you visit, do so in the summer; you are far to the north and snow is slow to melt.

BRIDGE (Cassia)

Bridge was a small farm and ranch town; today it is mostly a small cluster of abandoned buildings. Bridge got its start as a stagecoach station on a line that ran daily from Albion to Kelton. The stagecoach would exchange mail and passengers at Bridge while the horse team was watered and rested. Soon, Bridge grew into a small town. The stage was still running in the early 1900s, and when it stopped agriculture became the town's only industry. Natural hot water wells were drilled here. They were used to provide both water and heat for greenhouses.

A post office was built at Bridge in 1880. It was a log cabin and its first postmaster was Lee Kirk. Timber for building had to be hauled from the Jim Sage Mountains, which lay to the west of town. The first post office was replaced in the 1890s with a new building, another log cabin. This second building served as the town's post office until at least 1969. Its postmaster, Frank Olson, was a WWI vet who had been wounded in the Argonne Forest.

The town also had a school. It was much needed. The next closest one was ten miles south at the ranch community of Stanrod. Stanrod is on the Idaho-Utah border, and it too is a small ghost town. The first school at Bridge, like all the other buildings, was a log cabin. A much newer one-room schoolhouse and its outdoor bathrooms

The sign says it all.

Bridge School. The next closest school was more than ten miles away.

replaced it and stand abandoned today. Building materials and techniques here show construction in three different time periods, each a decade apart. There are at least ten vacant buildings at this site. Bridge is south of Malta and just west of Highway 81.

CARRIETOWN (Camas)

This was a small silver mining town deep in the Little Smoky Mountain Mining District. It is in southeast Camas County about twenty miles northwest of Hailey. At its peak, the population reached somewhere between three hundred to seven hundred, probably closer to the lower end. The town started during the early 1870s and flourished into the late 1880s. It was located at the headwaters of Carrie Creek. The principal mine here was the Carrie Leonard Mine, hence the name Carrietown.

Most of the buildings that remain here—and there are few—appear to postdate the site's history, so it was probably reoccupied. My guess—and this is only a guess—is the 1930s. The buildings lay in a cluster north of National Forest Road #227, aka the Warm Springs Creek Road. Most are in bad condition, although you can still see some had been converted from their original use. A couple structures are collapsed piles of wood. Simple log construction was mostly used. The location is just over the Camas/Blaine County line and on the west side of the Smoky Mountains, so you must cross over a mountain pass. The road here is a little rough. Elevation at the site is around 9,000 feet.

This area is near Sun Valley and is now popular with summer campers and hikers. A large forest fire raged through the woods all around Ketchum during late August 2007.

To check for location, road conditions, or to obtain the correct topo map, drop in the Sawtooth National Recreation Area Visitor Center north of Ketchum on Highway 75.

Some of the few structures standing at Bridge are quite old. The timber to build these had to be hauled in from the mountains in the background.

CHESTERFIELD (Caribou)

The Chesterfield area was first settled during 1875 by stragglers from Oregon Trail wagon trains. The trail ran through the valley. The community did not take hold, and these first settlers moved on. In 1880, Mormons moved into this valley and set up a temporary camp. During spring 1881, these Mormon settlers moved from their camp within the valley to the present-day location of Chesterfield.

The town was formally named Chesterfield on November 27, 1883. A large, prosperous farm community grew in the valley and, combined with traffic from the Oregon Trail, caused the business sector of the town to flourish. For a while there were plans to bring a railroad through the valley, but the railroad company chose a different route. Eventually traffic from the Oregon Trail dried up. Roads bypassed the valley, and drought, lightning, locusts and prairie fires took their toll on the farm community.

Chesterfield is at the end of the Chesterfield Road, about fifteen miles north of U.S. Highway 30 at Bancroft. The road to this location is well marked and paved. Mixed into the site are a few active farms. A small number of buildings have been rebuilt and are open to the public. Other buildings are being restored by Mormon missionaries. A few families that trace their roots to Chesterfield still hold family picnics and reunions here. There is little shade. The same lack of trees that makes shade rare makes lightning a not-so-rare problem. This is a dangerous strike zone. A good number of buildings in this town have burned down, some more than once, due to lightning strikes.

The town is easy to find, historical, partially restored, picturesque, and on a good road. In short, it is a rare gem.

DIXIE (Idaho)
ALTITUDE 5,600 FEET

Two miners struck placer gold in Dixie Gulch on August 24, 1862, but lost their claim due to Indian hostilities. A second party that

First: If the weather is good, Chesterfield is a wonderful place to visit.

Second: Notice the two different-era gas pumps. The business is closed but in excellent condition.

Third: The schools at Chesterfield have been repeatedly struck by lightning.

Fourth: The Mormon Church at Chesterfield.

season found gold but got lost and couldn't find their strike again. The next prospectors came through the area during 1864 or the 1870s, depending on the source. The second strike led to the settlement of Dixie. Its name comes from an early settler. It grew slowly, and most of the population left every winter. Unlike other mining towns in the area, Chinese were not allowed to live there during Dixie's boom days. A post office was established in fall 1896. A wagon road was completed from Elk City in 1897.

Mining, business and population went up and down. In 1892 the town had dwindled to a grand total of one. In 1901 the town was booming. Every building was full and tents had popped up like spring flowers. Another burst would occur in the 1920s and one more in the 1930s.

Dixie is located in the center of the state, twenty-six miles south of Elk City. The road into town is an all-weather one. The services here are limited to one store with a pay phone. It is also the post office and gas station. The population varies with the seasons. There are numerous original structures with many converted from their original use. Mines and mining equipment extend for miles in all directions. Many claims are still active.

When my 2007 field research trip was over, Dixie was in the path of a forest fire. The town was under an evacuation order and the buildings were being wrapped in a sort of foil. When the fall snows extinguished the fire, Dixie was still standing.

FLORENCE (Idaho)
ALTITUDE APPROXIMATELY 6,000 FEET

This was a community of some longevity, numerous phases, and much history. According to most accounts, it started when five prospectors broke off from a much larger group of men who were returning to California after having prospected farther north the previous season. This smaller group discovered a rather large placer deposit. The place, now called Florence Basin, was a bonanza. For miles, all the creeks, banks, and even fields contained gold dust.

These rich deposits covered an area more than twenty-five square miles! This was probably in late August 1861. In a couple weeks, the five grew to fifty. By November 1, there were one thousand stampeders. This ragged bunch was spread out in tents over a four- to six-square-mile area called Millersburg. Sometime during November, the miners held a meeting to organize a township. It was decided to lay out a miner's town on Summit Flat at the upper reaches of Baboon Gulch. It was also decided to change the name of the place to Florence.

There are many conflicting stories on the origin of this name. One story is that it was the name of the adopted daughter of Dr. Ferber. He was a popular area pioneer and town doctor. Another story is that it was the name of a popular madam or soiled dove of the town. Yet one more story is that the town was named for Florence Hunt. She was the daughter of Jim and Julie Hunt. Jim was a grocer and hotel owner in the new town. Reportedly, Florence was the first child born to the community.

Top: I found only a half dozen log structures remaining at Florence.

Bottom: All structures I found were in extremely poor condition. The photo in the National Forest pamphlet shows this site ten years ago, and the place has deteriorated badly since.

The winter started out mild, and miners continued to pour in until there were as many as three thousand. Then, just before Christmas, the weather turned bad and stayed that way until well into the summer. In fact, there was a huge blizzard in Central Idaho during July 2–5, 1862, which hit Florence on the 3rd. During the town's first winter, it had more snow than food. It snowed for 113 days that winter. The snow was so deep that it kept food from being packed in. The miners suffered from freezing and snow blindness. Many nearly starved and were forced to eat their mules or even such things as their own leather belts. In late spring 1862, the town was moved to the agreed-upon site on Summit Flat, and the first location was then worked for its placer deposits.

Getting supplies into Florence was difficult. Grangerville to the northwest and White Bird to the southwest were the principal supply bases for this rush. The only way to the gold fields was by rough trails, and these had to be hacked through a mountain wilderness first.

During 1863–64, Florence boomed with miners, merchants, and crime. One boomer managed to sell a store made of rough lumber and with no inventory for $2,500. Estimates of the population here ranged from five thousand to nine thousand. The whole site resembled a disturbed ant mound with thousands of people moving about and many more of them digging at the ground. Thousands of campfires gave the place an eerie glow and filled the basin with smoke.

The town site grew rapidly, with the Florence sawmill providing much of the material. There was a Masonic hall, dance hall, butcher shop, bakery, post office, meat market, newspaper, stagecoach office, livery, Wells Fargo office, Clark's Hotel plus two others, a Chinese laundry and a white laundry, stores, and saloons. The town had Idaho's first county courthouse and first public school. It was built in spring 1864 and consisted of an eight-by-twelve-foot log cabin.

By fall 1865, the town had dwindled to just one person. From then to summer 1869, mining here was done only during the summer and then on a small scale. The county seat was moved to the town of Washington that year. Then, a large Chinese population moved in and reworked the old claims from 1869 to 1880. When the Chinese left, Florence died. It had a rebirth in 1895, when quartz mining started here. The leading mine to push this boom was the Waverly. It operated from 1896 to 1939. Others were the Lone Pine, Bullion, and Yakima. There was a disagreement between the owners of the vacant Florence town site and the new mine developers, so in 1896, a third site was chosen for the town. It covered forty acres with mostly tents and rough-hewn log structures. Many structures here were disassembled for their building material or moved whole from

Other remains dot the Basin. These might be the rib-remains of a good dredge.

old Florence to the new location. This was easy; the new location was only a half mile south of old Florence. Then, they mined the soil of the old town site for gold dust. Just like in the movie *Paint Your Wagon*, gold dust had fallen through the cracks in the floorboards in these old buildings. One improvement: this time they built a jail.

During this rush, the peak population in 1897 was one thousand. This boom lasted through 1899, and after that began another yet slower decline. By 1900, only a few small stamp mills continued operations. During the 1930s, there was one more small rush. Two reasons: higher gold prices and new technology. The new technology was dragline dredging. You can still see the dredge ponds there today. Finally in 1940, the town had dwindled to just ten people, and a few individuals were doing mining in the basin. Eventually, Florence became vacant a second time. An old-time woman prospector bought both town sites and tried mining under them yet one more time. Her technique: burn down the old structures, then sluice the ashes and dirt below.

Today, there is not much left of Florence. The location you see is the third one even if some of the structures are older and from the second town location. The National Forest brochure says there are a dozen buildings. I found only a half dozen, all in poor shape and resembling nothing like the cabin shown in the brochure from a 1997 photo. Other evidence of the mining boom is spread thinly over the Basin. Water-diversion ditches and mining trenches crisscross the area. I found the bare wooden ribs of a gold dredge sticking up out of a bog.

Florence's final location is marked on the Nez Perce National Forest map. The road to Florence is marked with numerous signs. Don't follow them; follow the map. The signs bring you in a southern route, and it turned out to be a four-wheel drive road. I hiked the last four and a half miles in. The northern route the map takes is a better road.

First: Gnome has the look of a company town.
Second: This house had the rare luxury of a railed front porch.
Third: This building was probably a school.
Fourth: Another hazard in ghost town hunting—abandoned wells.

Most of the land here is National Forest, but some private property is mixed in. Stay out of the abandoned mines; they are extremely dangerous. One more thing to keep your eyes open for: this is moose country. The cemetery is a mile north of town. The National Forest Service has a historical marker at both the cemetery and the town site.

GNOME (Idaho)
ALTITUDE 3,460 FEET

Gnome is unique. It was a town that flourished during the Great Depression. Gold prices soared during the Depression, and Gnome was a place where there was gold. The community got its name from the Gnome Mine. This was an underground hard-rock mine that produced gold and silver ore. The mine operated from 1932 to 1937 and produced between ten thousand and forty thousand tons of ore. Dredges working Crooked River at the time also produced placer gold. The dredge tailings are still there today. Gnome had a cyanide mill with a twenty-five-ton-a-day capacity. In addition, there was a mine office, an assay office, mine buildings, a bunkhouse, a school, and a small number of homes for family men. The town had the modern amenities of phone and electric, although these were actually hooked up to very few buildings, and most of these belonged to the mine. Still, at this time, jobs were hard to come by, and those working here were probably just happy to have a job and a roof. They also had the use of the Orogrande airstrip, which is just a couple of miles south on Crooked River Road.

Gnome is located southwest of Elk City on the Crooked River Road. The location is shown on the Nez Perce National Forest map. The town rests on the east side of the road. A historical sign marks the site.

The dredge tailings here make the Crooked River look more like a gravel quarry than a mountain stream. An old dredge lay stranded here until the early 1990s, when it was moved to Oregon. The location is still marked on some maps. What you find at the location are dredge tailings, a historical marker, and the fallen remains of a mill. Remains of Gnome include the school, mine office, other mine buildings, cabins, and outhouses.

HENRY (Caribou)

This is a location I stumbled across. Many ghost towns in my books are not to be found in other books or websites. There are a fair number of sites I have come upon during my travels or studies of the area in question. Henry is one of these.

In 1892, William J. Chester built and opened the Henry store. It sold supplies to local ranchers and may have been a stagecoach stop. A small community grew up around the store.

The Henry store remained open well into the late twentieth century selling food and supplies to tourists and outdoorsmen. The creation of the Blackfoot Reservoirs brought more business to the store. An RV campground and a boat ramp sit right across state Highway 34 from the Henry store. There are eight intact buildings and sheds, along with one ancient wooden grain silo. A mobile home sits behind the old store.

This location is marked on road atlases and state highway maps. Approximately fifteen miles northwest of Henry on state Highway 34 is the nearby semi-ghost town of Wayan.

HOLBROOK (Oneida)

Holbrook is a semighost town in southern Idaho. After having established themselves in Utah, Mormons started to expand to neighboring states. This movement led to a small number of Mormon farm towns being established in southern Idaho; Holbrook was one of these. It was first settled in 1897. In 1901, the town acquired a post office, and the community was given the name Holbrook. The name comes from the town's first postmaster and its first bishop, Heber A. Holbrook.

Besides the post office, the town had a school, a general store, and a Latter-Day Saints church. On my visit, a group of volunteers was fixing up the old church and doing quite a good job of it. They were very polite and friendly and were nice enough to put up with all my questions. The main farm crop here was wheat. Some potatoes were also grown. Mormons introduced potatoes to Idaho.

Top: The Henry general store.

Middle: The buildings here are well preserved but still show their age. The structure in the background is a small wooden grain silo.

Bottom: This small school or church is at the back of the RV park. Notice the two electrical hookups on either side of the building.

Today, Holbrook is quiet and much smaller than it used to be. On a walk around town, I saw old blocks of streets with sidewalks laid out, but all the buildings were gone. There were two vacant businesses, one abandoned grain silo, and a small, clean city park to see here. A small number of vacant old frame homes existed. There is also a small population, so be respectful of property rights. The town is on a paved road and still shown on the state highway map.

HUMPHREY (Clark)

Off Interstate 15 at Exit 190 are the remains of the small town of Humphrey. There are no services here, no trees, no shade, and only two original buildings. What there is plenty of is wind. The town site has been bought up and is now part of a ranch. All property here is private and posted, so be respectful. Do not stop on the interstate. Get off the highway, legally park your vehicle, and view the leisurely way on foot.

What is left here is an old school and a house. The school and its play yard are currently being used as part of a stock pen. The residence is still used and has an outhouse complete with a crescent moon carved in the door. On my visit, there was also a sheepherder's wagon in the front yard.

A study of old maps showed that a Union Pacific rail line ran through here. For decades, this town had been marked on all state highway maps and highway atlases, but recently it has disappeared. The town was here before the interstate. Construction of the highway went through the center of the site and would have taken a lot of the town with it.

HUNT STATION (Jerome)

This is the name of a train station that was at one time used as a transfer point for Japanese Americans being sent to the Minidoka Relocation Center. Often, the camp was actually referred to by the train station name instead of its official name. Sometimes it was simply called "Hunt Camp" or just "Hunt." The camp operated from August 16, 1942, to October 26, 1945. At its peak, it held ten thousand Japanese Americans. More than one thousand from this camp ended up serving in the U.S. military during WWII. Most joined either 442nd Infantry Regiment and the 100th Infantry Battalion. These two outfits were among the most decorated

Top: The Humphrey School.

Middle: The only other intact building at Humphrey. Notice the sheepherder's wagon at right.

Left: This sentry station was built of volcanic rock.

American units in WWII. They also had two of the highest casualty rates during the war. The camp closed on October 26, 1945, and it immediately became the largest ghost town in Idaho.

The camp covered more than 950 acres and was laid out like an army base, except that it was surrounded by barbed wire and armed guards. It owed its existence to President Franklin Delano Roosevelt and his signing of Executive Order 9066. The Democrat Party icon had argued, "The successful prosecution of the war requires every possible protection against espionage and sabotage." A total of ten internment camps were authorized and located in the western interior of the country, mostly on Native American lands. The camps had schools, libraries, theaters, and much more, just like any other American town their size. Still, living conditions were difficult. Internees could work outside of camp but had to have a permit. The environment in which most of the camps were located was harsh. These places were boiling hot in the summer, bone-chilling cold in the winter, and always full of sand or dust. Living spaces in the camps were cramped, and boredom was a constant companion. The location was remote. The next closest town was sixty miles away.

A historical sign on State Highway 24 east of Shoshone marks the location of the former train station. The actual campsite was just north of the Hunt Station. There is another marker and the stone remains of the post gate, a waiting room, and a guard station. Interestingly, the waiting room and guard station were made of volcanic rock. More remains are scattered over a wide area, with most being converted to farm or ranch use.

IDIMON (Clark)

This was a small farming and ranch community. Construction shows it was occupied over an extended period of time. Today it is totally vacant. Its location is fourteen miles east of Spencer, Idaho, on Kilgore Road. A historical sign in Spencer will pinpoint its location for you.

Top: Although numerous barracks and other buildings from the camp still stand today, they are hard to recognize because they have been converted to other uses.

Bottom: Downtown Idimon.

The construction spans different time periods. For example, there are at least three different kinds of roofs here. The first buildings were built of logs and rough-hewn timbers. The wood had to be hauled in from the mountains to the north. A newer structure of cinder blocks appears to have been a school. It was bisected into large rooms. Maybe the school was being divided as boy/girl. Chalkboards on the walls are what told me this was probably a school. Abandoned cabins and old farm equipment litter the fields for some distance.

This town started during the mid-1880s. It supplied beef and farm produce to the booming mines at Spencer and elsewhere. The town would have also provided services to the local farmers and ranchers.

Respect and do not touch any of the structures here. This is private property.

MORROW (Lewis)

This was a small but important country town. It started along the banks of Willow Creek as the Morrow Stage Station in the late 1800s. Later, it grew into a town, and the name morphed into Morrow Town.

This town served local farmers and ranchers and competed with nearby West Lula for their business. Early in the 1900s, the stage line went out of business. The barn for the stagecoach became the town livery. During the early 1900s, it was converted into a dance hall, and Morrow Town became an important social center. By this time, the place was simply called Morrow. Both the closing of the dance hall and the Depression hit the town hard. When highways and railroads bypassed Morrow, it faded away.

Today, all there is to remind us is a road sign by that name and a barn along Willow Creek. About a mile to the east are the remains of the old farm community of West Lake.

This building had two main rooms, each with a wall-length chalkboard, hence I guessed it was a school.

A barn and maybe the old dance hall of Morrow.

There were still dishes and silverware on the tables of the café.

NAF (Cassia)

Naf is a tiny, attractive, and recently abandoned ranch community. John Naf, who was also the town's first postmaster, settled the town in the 1890s. The first post office was located on Naf's homestead about a half mile south, just over the Utah border. There was also a log schoolhouse here in the pioneer days. At that time, the settlement's name was Clear Creek. When they applied for the post office, it was rejected under that name because there was another Clear Creek in southern Utah, so the name was changed to Naf.

The town layout is basically a strip of business buildings at the top of a T-shaped road intersection. Buildings here are old but well maintained. The Naf store was built before the 1920s. The post office is about seventy years old. The old log schoolhouse is still standing, although modified and painted over. Across the street from the store is a dance hall. It was built in 1946 and is still occasionally used. There is also a café, gas station, a few homes, and various sheds and outbuildings. Nearby are the other ghost town sites of Bridge and Strevell.

Naf is located on a desert prairie with a beautiful mountain range for a background.

OVID (Bear Lake)
ALTITUDE 5,993 FEET

Ovid was founded as a Danish farm community. The first settlers arrived during summer 1863, but they wintered in the nearby community of Paris. They returned in spring 1864 and started a permanent community. The town was named after a Roman poet.

The settlement was located in a lush valley. There was good grass and plenty of water, but the wind and winters here are harsh. The first permanent business structure was a general merchandise store run and owned by A. E. Sorenson. Due to local Indian scares, a fort was built here in summer 1864.

Today the Ovid school occupies the site. By the late 1880s, the town had become a Mormon community. A Mormon church was finished here in 1896. It still stands today minus its steeple. A school, post office, and two blacksmith shops operated, but the town had no bank or newspaper.

Ovid is located at the intersection of Highways 36 and 89. The location is marked on the state highway map.

Top: The Mormon Church.
Middle: Part of Ovid's old business district.
Left: The Ovid School has been converted into a private residence.

PEARL (Gem)

Pearl was a gold mining community that had its beginning in the late 1860s. It started on December 7, 1867, when a local rancher showed up in nearby Boise with some good-looking ore specimens. The samples had been taken from the substantial-looking quartz-bearing veins located on Willow Creek. The veins were well defined and only two hundred feet apart. They were separated by Willow Creek and ran parallel to each other and the creek. This would mean there was pay dirt within the streambed, too! Still, development in Willow Creek Gulch was slow. Hard-rock mining is expensive and difficult, especially in undeveloped wilderness areas like 1867 Idaho. Also, Willow Creek is usually dry, so this made it more challenging to recover the placer deposits in the creek bed.

At first, miners hoped to build a reservoir at the head of Willow Creek Gulch to provide water for placer mining. This did not succeed. During 1870, some hard-rock mining was attempted with the opening of the Red Warrior mine. After a limited amount of work, the mine closed the same year. Pearl was mostly dormant the next couple of decades. In 1894, gold mining and the town both boomed due to a spike in gold prices. After 1900, rising development and mining costs slowed the rush to a crawl; by 1908, it stopped. Several attempts over the decades to develop and extend Pearl's largest mine, the Lincoln, were not productive. By 1945, the town had faded away.

The town was strung out in the bottom of a gulch along Willow Creek, where the little that remains today can be found. Foundations, mine adits, a cabin or two, loading ramps, debris, and more are scattered for a couple of miles along Pearl Creek Road. I had approached from Highway 55 and found, to my displeasure, that stretches of Pearl Creek Road were nothing better than a mud trough.

Top: The eastern approach to Pearl. Parts of this road had become a mud trough.

Middle: One of the mines at Pearl—stay out!

Bottom: Remains of a log-constructed ore bin.

This is the most intact structure at Sawtooth City.

SAWTOOTH CITY (Blaine)

Named for the beautiful mountains that overshadow it, this was a gold and silver mining boomtown. A lode deposit was discovered nearby on June 4, 1879, at a place that would come to be called Vienna. With the impending rush, additional discoveries were made, and another town came into being late that summer on Beaver Creek. At a miners' meeting on November 29, 1879, the town was formally christened Sawtooth City. A post office was established on September 30, 1880. Supplies had to be packed in, and this slowed development. Later, developers would run into fuel, processing, and technological problems.

At first ore was packed out over the mountains so it could be milled in Atlanta. Still, by August 1881, the place was booming with more than a dozen businesses and a population of six hundred. By that fall, it had grown to one thousand people. The business sector here grew to at least five saloons, three general stores, two meat markets,

Most of Sawtooth City now looks like this. Gathering firewood at this site is not permitted.

three restaurants, a tailor shop, two other stores, at least one hotel, a livery stable, an assay office, a blacksmith shop, a Chinese laundry, and a stagecoach station for the line to Ketchum. There were only about thirty cabins at the time, so many must have lived in boardinghouses, tents, or their businesses. By late summer 1882, a stamp mill was running here. In 1883, the Columbia and Beaver Company built a twenty-stamp mill a short way above the town. All that remains of the Columbia Mill is its stone foundation. In 1884, a concentrator was installed, and business picked up even more. The town was probably at its peak. Another mill and a bunkhouse were located at the Silver King Mine two miles up Beaver Creek.

The boom lasted through summer 1889. The town lost its post office in 1890. Most people left that winter, but some stayed into 1892. On August 9 of that year, a shaft fire destroyed much equipment of the last major mine there. It was the Silver King, the most productive and consistently active mine of the rush. This put an end to Sawtooth City. It had suffered from the usual problems for central Idaho mining towns: isolation, poor transportation, hard winters, and high development costs.

The town is located south of Alturas Lake and about four miles west of U.S. Highway 93 on National Forest Road #204, aka Beaver Creek Road. I took a van to this location, but the road is rutted and should be driven only when it is dry and cleared of snow.

The law does not permit gathering firewood at this site. Construction here was with logs, and it is next to impossible to tell if you're gathering parts of an old building. Remains cover a fairly large area. It is easy to see much of the layout of the old town site. Streets were laid out in straight, square lines and can still be seen. Disintegrated, littered remains show the outlines of numerous log cabins and buildings. Numerous pits show where basements and outhouses once were. One sad sight was several standing empty frames that once contained historical markers. Now they stand silent, with their treasure of information lost to time. This site used to show on numerous maps and atlases as a historical site or ghost town; now it is a ghost of a ghost.

Sawtooth City Cemetery is two miles away to the northeast on a barren hillside. Both the cemetery and town are protected historical sites. No souvenir hunting or open fires are permitted at either location, please.

You can still see the driveway leading up to the front door.

Top: This is all that remains of a gas station still open for business in 1982.

Bottom: While beautiful, the environment at Strevell is harsh and made living at this place a challenge.

STREVELL (Cassia)

This is a late-twentieth-century ghost town. Still, for being so recent, very little remains. It is still marked on numerous maps, is on a good paved road, and the route to it is well marked. These are some of the same reasons so little remains of it.

Salt Lake City businessmen established it in 1911 as a Union Pacific railroad boomtown. The railroad never made it to this town. Strevell was the name of one of the businessmen. The environment here is desert prairie, and at first, drinking water had to be delivered from Dive Springs in Utah. Despite these obstacles, the town grew as a business center for homesteaders, horsemen, and freight wagons. When roads come to the area, business picked up rapidly. The town boomed and became the social center for the area. Farmers came from many miles around to watch or play baseball. There were also dances and orchestras at a local hotel. It was a two-story building that included a dining room with a dance floor and a huge lobby with a large fireplace.

Other businesses were a barber, blacksmith shop, and general store, a repair garage, a couple of restaurants, three gas stations, tourist cabins, and the Mountain Springs Creamery. The town had a post office, red brick schoolhouse, baseball diamond, airfield, a small number of homes, and a truck weigh station. Most of the businesses had an attached residence. In isolated towns like this, most businesspeople would have to live at or very near their establishment. One near-famous business in Strevell was Mary's Café, which was well known, through truckers across the country for its homemade pies.

The road to Strevell is well marked, but the site isn't. Road signs constantly remind you how many miles to Strevell, but there is no sign when you finally arrive. There isn't much left for a sign to mark. Due to squatters, vandals, property taxes, and fear of lawsuit, the whole town site was leveled. It had been alleged that the hotel was haunted by a man who had hanged himself in the building.

The town had been located on a paved state highway, but when I-84 was built in the early 1890s, it bypassed Strevell, and the truck weight station was moved to the new road. The town faded amazingly fast, but it stayed around a lot longer on maps than it did in reality. It was often marked on highway maps as a ghost town, but now it is mostly a memory—from a town to almost dust in just twenty-five years. A few foundations and debris are about the only thing left here. On my first visit, there was one squatter with about a dozen anti-government signs. When I passed back through at the end of the summer, the squatter and his signs were gone. I was told he had been arrested—no one knew for what, and I didn't confirm his fate.

What's left of Strevell is on Highway 81 near the border with Utah. It is a desert environment here. Nearby are the additional ghost towns of Bridge and Naf.

TOLL GATE (Elmore)

This place is a tiny abandoned highway hamlet. It got its start in 1868 on a wagon road as a rest stop and toll station, hence the name Toll Gate.

Gold had been found in Idaho early, but transportation difficulties due to terrain were the norm. In 1869, Julius Newberg built the South Boise Road to the gold strike at Rocky Bar, Idaho. Steep grades on the Syrup Creek section caused hauling difficulties, so an alternate route was built through Rattlesnake Creek Canyon. This is the road that Toll Gate is on. Today the road is State Highway 20. The position at the entrance of the canyon made it a neutral place to set up a toll station. James A. Porter built a hotel and dairy here. The toll station operated for twenty years. Later, when the highway came, the place would become a rest stop for people with autos instead of wagons.

Today the place is totally abandoned and for sale. There are a little more than a half dozen standing and intact buildings here. In the

Top: Another Idaho ghost town for sale. The calendar in the café said June 1984.

Middle: There are a few buildings in a small gulch behind the businesses lined up along the highway.

Bottom: All I know is what the sign says.

café, a calendar behind the service counter still reads June 2001. My first visit was during July 2005. The structures are from different time periods stretching over decades, but they are suffering from the unwanted attention of roadside vandals. In addition to the buildings here, there is a State Highway historical sign. Toll Gate is situated eleven miles north of Mountain View.

WESTLAKE (Idaho)
ALTITUDE 4,604 FEET

Westlake started in the late 1800s as an overnight stage stop on the old Cottonwood Trail between Grangerville and Lewiston. Today the remains of this small agricultural community are to be sought among a maze of gravel farm roads.

The town was named after an early settler, Sarah Westlake. A store was built there in 1889. Westlake was awarded a post office in 1893. In addition to business traffic, the town provided services to local ranchers and farmers and traded with the nearby Nez Perce Indian Reservation. By 1910, there was the Westlake Hotel, a church,

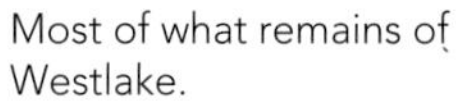

Most of what remains of Westlake.

other businesses, and more than fifty homes. The population then was 209. By 1920, the town was slowly fading. Bypassed by both highway and railroad, it would eventually be bypassed by time.

The business section of town is entirely gone except for a historical marker. What you do find are a few old homes that were at the edge of town.

The last of the business section folded during 1951. All that remains of it is a historical marker at the edge of a hayfield. There are a few vacant homes and farm buildings left three-tenths of a mile up the road. These structures are from two different eras. One residence and its outbuildings are late twentieth century; the rest are much older with shake shingle roofs.

The farm buildings start at the intersection of the West Lake and Morrow Town Roads and run east for about one-third mile.

About a mile to the west on the Morrow Town Road is the ghost town site of Morrow. These towns were competitors for local businesses, and they suffered equal fates.

The only resident of Westlake I found to interview.

BIBLIOGRAPHY

Today much research is done via the Internet. I used every source I could find. One of the better ones, in my opinion, is by Gary B. Speck: http://freepages.history.rootsweb.com/~gtusa/index.htm. Ghost town website http://www.ghosttowns.com/ and its members were an invaluable source as well.

Other sources used include, but are not limited to, the following:

Bowen, J. *Legendary Towns of the Old West.* New York: Mallard Press, 1990.

Bower, D. *Ghost Towns & Back Roads.* Harrisburg: Stackpole Co., 1971.

Carter, W. *Ghost Towns of the West.* Menlo Park: Lane Magazine & Book Company, 1971.

Delorme. *Atlas of Idaho.* Yarmouth: Delorme, 2002.

Florin, Lambert. Western Ghost Towns. Seattle: Superior, 1961.

__________. *Boot Hill.* Seattle: Superior, 1966.

Miller, Donald C. *Ghost Towns of Idaho.* Boulder: Pruett, 1976.

O'Connor, J. *Rock Mountain Treasures.* Bend: Maverick, 1988.

Reader's Digest. "Off the Beaten Path." Pleasantville, 1987.

Schmidt, J and Thomas Schmidt. *The Smithsonian Guides to Natural America—The Northern Rockies.* Washington: Smithsonian Books, 1995.

Sparling, W. *Southern Idaho Ghost Towns.* Caldwell: Caxton, 1974.

Topping, G. *Ghost Towns of the Old West.* New York: Mallard Press, 1992.

Wallace, R. *The Miners.* New York: Time-Life Books, 1976.

Weis, Norman D. *Ghost Towns of the Northwest.* Caldwell: Caxton, 1971.

Wells, M. *Gold Camps & Silver Cities.* Moscow: University of Idaho Press, 2002.

Wolle, M. *The Bonanza Trail.* Indiana Press: Crown, 1952.

INDEX

Postscript

The Search

Pack trains of mules still take supplies to mountain mining camps in Idaho.

One day I'll scale the peaks in search of El Dorado.
Where is this place lost in wilderness I must go?
It lies within the painted veil,
A place many search and most will fail.

Where towering mountains meet the mist
But claim by many to be a myth.

Where lightning and hail dance with the snow
Above the line where the Blue Spruce grow.

Where the colors of the rainbow race across the sky.
The howling winds scream without ever asking why.
Many wonder what makes the rainbow glow,
Some even try to find from where it grows.

Hearts of some ache and feel they must know,
Even if it means they may lose their soul.

What is it that lies at the end of the rainbow?
The shine of gold or finally, the sight of El Dorado.

by Bruce A. Raisch

Does it really exist after all?

This sign marks the Nez Perce Pass. From here I took a week to cross Idaho's McGruder Corridor, solo.

ABOUT THE AUTHOR

Bruce A. Raisch, adventurer, ghost town hunter, historian and photographer, was born in North Africa as an "Air Force brat." Following family tradition, he enlisted for military service. While still in high school, he joined the Missouri Army National Guard and served in a combat engineer battalion. There he volunteered for demolitions work. He would later volunteer for five state emergency deployments, five NCO schools and five overseas deployments including the first Gulf War. The primary duty station for these deployments was historic Jefferson Barracks.

Bruce's first camping trip was in the Colorado Rockies at the age of two. He still remembers his parents bathing him in a cold mountain stream. His family moved to Denver when he was four years old.

You may learn more about the author in his first two books, *Ghost Towns of Wyoming* and *Ghost Towns and Other Historical Sites of the Black Hills* and at his website www.theghosttownhunter.com.